IN THE PATH OF LEWIS AND CLARK

Traveling the Missouri

PETER LOURIE

Silver Burdett Press
Parsippany, New Jersey

4/1/97 To the Bigelows, Best wishes, Peter Lourie

To William Least Heat-Moon,
a great river companion

Author's Note: Punctuation and spelling in the journals of Lewis and Clark have been modernized, but sentence structure remains loyal to the original. The entry dates in the two journals have been made uniform for clarity. Also, the mileage and time of day in my own Missouri journal are approximations.

Published by Silver Burdett Press
A Division of Simon & Schuster
299 Jefferson Road, Parsippany, New Jersey 07054

Designed by Beth Santos Design

Manufactured in the United States of America
ISBN 0-382-39307-4 (LSB) 10 9 8 7 6 5 4 3 2 1
ISBN 0-382-39308-2 (PBK) 10 9 8 7 6 5 4 3 2 1

Library of Congress Cataloging in Publication Data
Lourie, Peter
In the path of Lewis and Clark: traveling the Missouri River/by Peter Lourie
p. cm.
Summary: Describes the author's trip up the Missouri River by canoe and motorboat and compares it to the Lewis and Clark Expedition. Includes index.
1. Missouri River—Description and travel—Juvenile literature. 2. Lourie, Peter—Journeys —Missouri River—Juvenile literature. 3. Lewis and Clark Expedition (1804-1806)— Juvenile literature. [1. Missouri River—Description and travel. 2. Lewis and Clark Expedition (1804-1806)] I. Title.
F598.L68 1996   96-3496
917.804'33—dc20   CIP   AC

The author has launched an Internet site for studying the rivers of the world. This is a place for students and teachers to conduct research about rivers—their history, their people, their ecology, and more. Classes studying rivers can communicate with each other and discuss their river studies at RiverResource.

http://www.highlands.com/RiverResource

Table of Contents

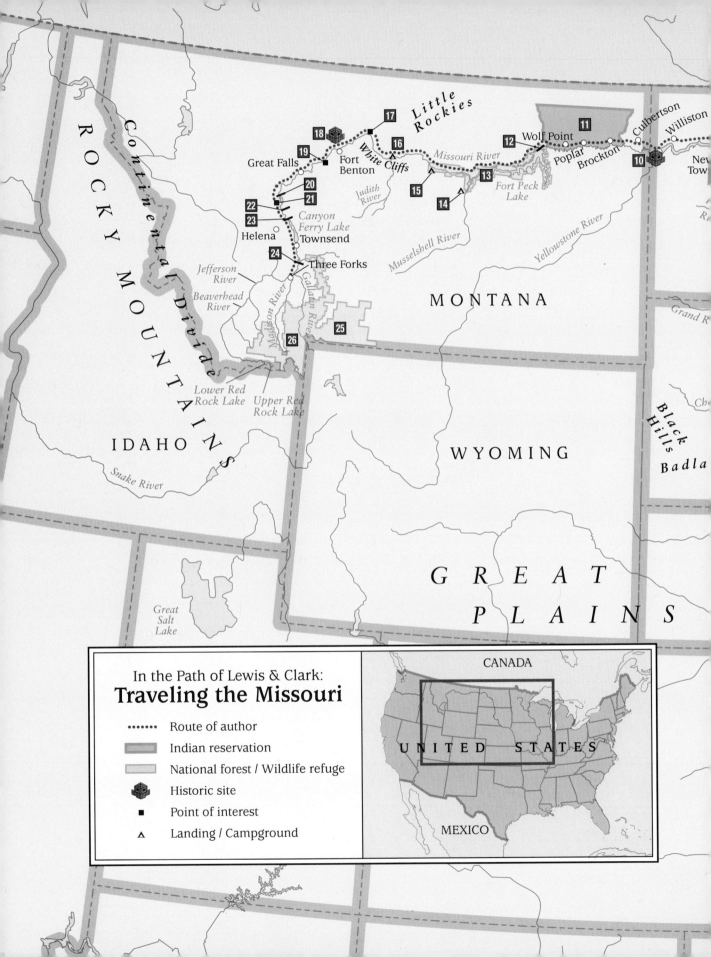

In the Path of Lewis & Clark:
Traveling the Missouri

- **••••••** Route of author
- Indian reservation
- National forest / Wildlife refuge
- Historic site
- Point of interest
- Landing / Campground

ROCKY MOUNTAINS

Continental Divide

Little Rockies

White Cliffs

Missouri River

MONTANA

Great Falls
Fort Benton
Helena
Townsend
Three Forks

Judith River

Canyon Ferry Lake

Musselshell River

Fort Peck Lake

Wolf Point
Poplar
Brockton
Culbertson
Williston
New Town

Jefferson River
Beaverhead River
Madison River
Gallatin River

Lower Red Rock Lake
Upper Red Rock Lake

IDAHO

Snake River

WYOMING

Yellowstone River

Black Hills
Badla

GREAT

PLAINS

Great Salt Lake

CANADA

UNITED STATES

MEXICO

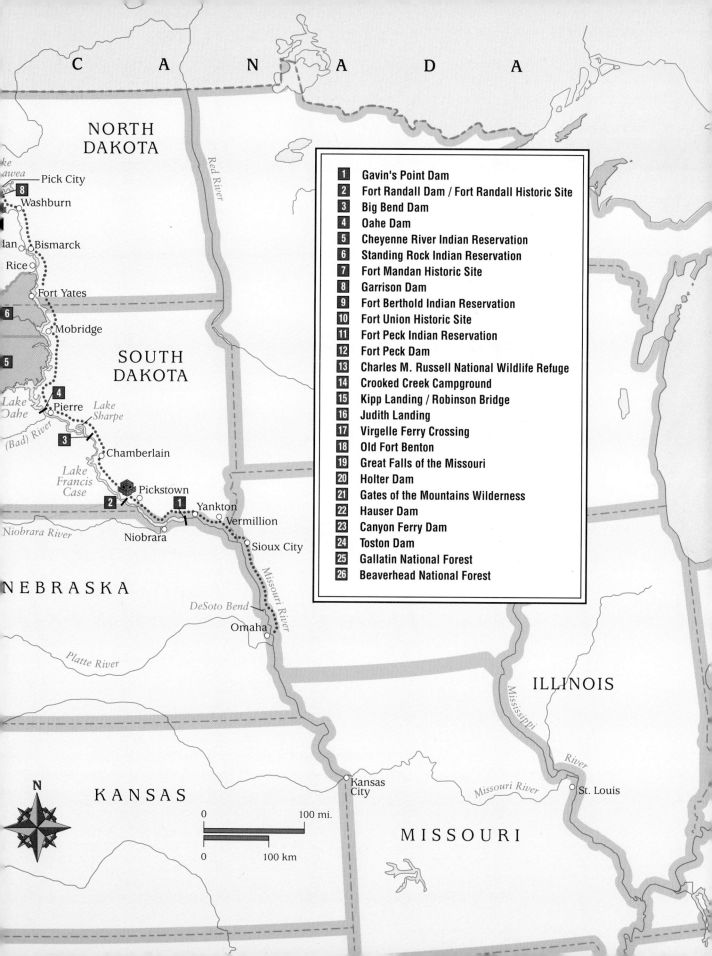

CANADA

NORTH DAKOTA

8 Pick City
Washburn

Bismarck
Rice

Fort Yates

6

Mobridge

SOUTH DAKOTA

5

4 Pierre
Lake Oahe
(Bad) River

Lake Sharpe

3

Chamberlain

Lake Francis Case

2 Pickstown

1 Yankton
Vermillion

Niobrara

Sioux City

NEBRASKA

Niobrara River

DeSoto Bend

Omaha

Missouri River

Platte River

ILLINOIS

Mississippi

River

N

KANSAS

Kansas City

Missouri River

St. Louis

MISSOURI

Red River

1	Gavin's Point Dam
2	Fort Randall Dam / Fort Randall Historic Site
3	Big Bend Dam
4	Oahe Dam
5	Cheyenne River Indian Reservation
6	Standing Rock Indian Reservation
7	Fort Mandan Historic Site
8	Garrison Dam
9	Fort Berthold Indian Reservation
10	Fort Union Historic Site
11	Fort Peck Indian Reservation
12	Fort Peck Dam
13	Charles M. Russell National Wildlife Refuge
14	Crooked Creek Campground
15	Kipp Landing / Robinson Bridge
16	Judith Landing
17	Virgelle Ferry Crossing
18	Old Fort Benton
19	Great Falls of the Missouri
20	Holter Dam
21	Gates of the Mountains Wilderness
22	Hauser Dam
23	Canyon Ferry Dam
24	Toston Dam
25	Gallatin National Forest
26	Beaverhead National Forest

0   100 mi.

0   100 km

Prologue

In 1995 the well-known writer William Least Heat-Moon made a remarkable journey. He traveled across the United States by boat. Starting where the tides of the Atlantic Ocean flood into the harbor of New York City, he finished his 5,400-mile trip where the Columbia River pours into the Pacific Ocean.

In order to make this trip, Heat-Moon used many of the rivers and waterways that once were the main highways of America—the Hudson, the Erie Canal, the Great Lakes, the Allegheny, the Ohio, the Mississippi, the Missouri, and the Columbia rivers. Of these great waterways, the Missouri is the longest river in the United States, forming almost half of Heat-Moon's entire transcontinental trip. It is also one of the most difficult rivers in the world to navigate.

Heat-Moon asked me and two other friends to help him with the Missouri leg of his journey. For 2,540 miles the Missouri cuts across seven states. Steamboat captains used to call it Old Misery, because the river changes course constantly and acts in swift, dangerous ways. Ahead of us lay shifting sandbars, drifting trees, whirlpools, and dams. Nothing worried Heat-Moon as much as the Missouri.

It worried me, too. As a travel writer, I've taken expeditions to remote places. I've lived on the Amazon River and searched for seven hundred tons of Incan gold in the Andean jungles of Ecuador. I've paddled the Yukon River to the goldfields of the Klondike. I once canoed the entire length of the Hudson River from its source in the Adirondack Mountains to the Atlantic Ocean. I have also spent time with the Miccosukee Indians in Florida's Everglades.

My favorite mode of travel is the canoe. Paddling quietly, I can really feel a river, see and hear it for the first time. Canoes would be a part of Heat-Moon's trip, too, but what worried me about the Missouri was the current. I had never traveled a river upstream before.

In 1803 France sold the Louisiana Territory to the United States, doubling the size of the country. In 1804 Captains Meriwether Lewis and William Clark set off to see what lay in this unmapped territory. President Thomas Jefferson ordered them to explore the Missouri River westward and to observe the Indians, minerals, animals, and climate of the unknown land. Lewis and Clark traveled by keelboat, canoe, and horseback. From 1804 to 1806, they covered more than eight thousand miles. Much of that time was spent on the Missouri River.

Once the great river highway to the west, the Missouri today is a forgotten river. It seldom makes the news unless it floods.

Lewis and Clark journey, 1804-1806

I wanted to see how much the Missouri had changed since the days of Lewis and Clark. What did the river look like today? Was it polluted? What role did the river play in the lives of people who lived there? On my tape recorder, I recorded notes about what I saw and heard while traveling 1,700 miles up the river. This is a modern-day Missouri River journal.

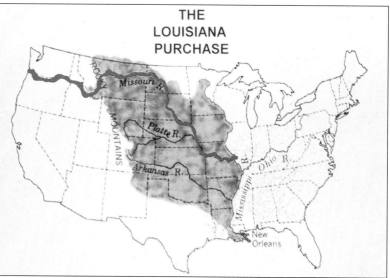

Nebraska

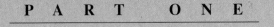

My First Day

May 28, 11:00 A.M. I put on my rain gear and prepare for a long, cold, wet first day. The sky threatens another big storm. The wind is gusting to thirty-five miles an hour out of the northwest. It's 55 degrees, rainy and misty. This is the same wet weather Bill Least Heat-Moon has faced for the past two weeks. The Missouri is having one of its worst floods in a century.

When I met him, I could tell Bill was at the end of his rope. He was bailing water from his boat with a plastic milk carton. I came right up to him and said, "So, can you use some help, Mister?"

He swung around and smiled. "Oh, thank goodness, it's you." I looked at the trees floating in the river and asked, "How do you dodge those?"

He said the big trees weren't so dangerous. "It's the small ones—the ones you can't see. Here. Look at this." Bill showed me a torn propeller, its blade twisted and jagged from hitting something. The sub-merged log—or whatever—was invisible. There was a bang and the motor kicked. He had to replace the prop before continuing upriver. Propellers are expensive. Bill has only a few props left. If he runs out, it might be the end of his trip, and mine, too.

Mile 616—upriver from the confluence of the Missouri and the Mississippi, N.P. Dodge Marina, Omaha, Nebraska

On facing page, Omaha skyline from the Missouri River. © Jeff Morgan; *below*, Bill bailing his boat

Our engines cut through the Big Muddy.

12:00 P.M. It's time for us to get on the river. Bill, dreading another battle with the flood, hesitates. Then with a sigh, he says, "Well, we better roll. I wish that wind would come down."

As we pull away from the dock I cast the tip of a deer antler into the water. It was a gift to me last year from an Abenaki Indian in Vermont. I offer it to the raging Missouri River with a prayer that our trip will be a successful one.

We plow into the swift current. The boat is jolted back as if reeling from a giant boxing glove. Bill guns the engines and we're off. The water is the color of milk chocolate, from all the earth it is carrying. The Sioux called the river "Mini Sose" (Mi-ni So-say), meaning muddy water. "Big Muddy" is one of the Missouri's many names.

Bill steers and I sit up front with him. I peer out at the water. That's my job today: I'm an extra pair of eyes. When I see something large coming our way, I say, "Log at one o'clock," meaning it's a little to the right of twelve, which is straight ahead. Often Bill must jerk the boat sharply to the right and then to the left.

For more than a year Bill searched for the perfect boat for his journey. The Missouri presented the biggest problem. With its famous shifting sandbars and snags (trees held fast underwater), the Missouri required a flat-hulled boat. A boat with a flat hull draws less water. That means it can pass over the river's shallow parts. Also, it can more easily be backed off

Above, The crew; *below*, Nikawa, our river horse

any unseen sandbar. Bill calls his boat the *Nikawa*, which means "river horse" in the Osage language. (Some of Bill's ancestors were Osage Indians.) Propelling the *Nikawa* against the current are two 45 horsepower Honda engines. They are quiet compared to most motors, but they are still noisy. Bill uses earplugs to muffle the constant drone. The *Nikawa* rolls and swerves when it hits the boils that erupt out of the brown liquid like giant bubbles. But the *Nikawa's* flat hull crosses the strong current more easily than a boat with a V-shaped hull.

With so many sandbars and snags, the Missouri made travel for Lewis and Clark extremely difficult. Until the steamboats started coming up the Missouri around 1820, traveling upstream required unbelievable physical endurance. Lewis and Clark used a fifty-five-foot keelboat. It could hold up to ten tons of cargo. Twenty to forty men pulled the keelboat with the use of a heavy rope, usually a thousand-foot line tied to the top of a thirty-foot mast. The long rope helped keep the boat away from shore. Its great height above the boat helped keep the rope off the bushes. When they couldn't tug it upstream, the men poled the keelboat, eight to ten men on each side with long poles, pushing their poles into the river bottom in unison, stepping from front to back, then running forward quickly to begin the process again. When the river was too deep, they rowed with oars. Sometimes the wind was just right to fill a square sail that could be set on the mast.

In the spring of 1804, Lewis and Clark and forty-two men poled, pulled, sailed, and rowed their keelboat up the Missouri River. They also traveled with two pirogues (flat-bottomed dugout canoes commonly used on inland waters). They covered fourteen to twenty miles a day.

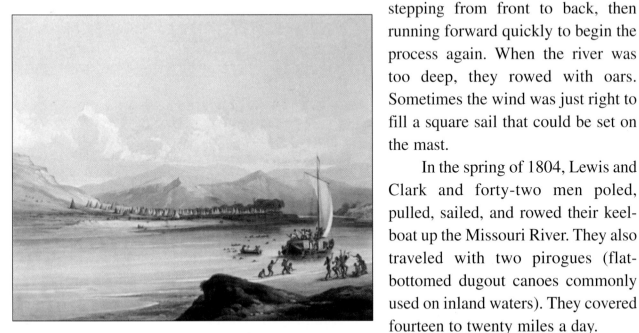

Karl Bodmer, "Camp of the Gros Ventres of the Prairies on the Upper Missouri." Joslyn Art Museum, Omaha, Nebraska, Gift of the Enron Art Foundation. (An example of a keel boat)

Our Missouri trip will have only four crew members. The other two, Bob Lindholm and Scott Buchanan, are at this minute driving the support vehicle, Bill's Ford Bronco, with the canoe and the *Nikawa's* trailer, to our next stop.

I'm sure glad we have two new motors on the *Nikawa* and a little one for the canoe. The canoe will be necessary for the shallower parts of the river. In the *Nikawa* we can go a hundred miles in a day. In the canoe, traveling five miles an hour against the current, we will probably make only thirty miles a day.

12:30 P.M. Bang! We've hit something. One engine isn't working right. It sends out a wild spray. Bill cuts the engines back a little. He swerves the boat from one side to the other, hoping the sticks, leaves, whatever, will come free of the propeller. I grab the wall of the cabin to keep from falling. Then he cuts the engines into neutral so we can inspect them. The mighty current slaps us around like a bar of soap in a bathtub. I lean way out over the water. It's okay. The snag has come free.

Bill guns it. This will be a long day. We might not get off the river until 8 or 9 P.M. My kids will be asleep, so I'll have to wait until tomorrow morning to speak to them.

I miss them already. It was so hard to say goodbye at the airport a few days ago. My two-year-old boy, Walker, latched onto my leg like a barnacle. He said, "Don't go. Don't go." Suzanna, who is six, could not stop crying. When I put Walker in the car, he sat staring at me icily. Then my wife Melissa drove away.

On the *Nikawa* Bill told me to travel light. But there were too many things I thought I needed: sleeping bag, air mattress, life jacket, small tent, rain gear, two shirts, two pairs of socks, two underwear, two long-sleeve shirts, sweater, sweatshirt, rain boots, sneakers, sandals, tin cup, plate, camera equipment, film, books (the journals of Lewis and Clark, of course),

Elkskin bound Field Journal of William Clark (1804-06). Missouri Historical Society, St. Louis.

tape recorder, tapes, notebooks, pens, batteries, flashlight, water bottle, hat, sunscreen, first-aid kit, and some candy bars for emergencies. When Bill saw my two big duffel bags, he was horrified.

Compared to the amount of equipment Lewis and Clark brought with them, I suppose I am traveling fairly light. For a two-year expedition, Lewis and Clark took literally tons of supplies. Camp equipment consisted of things like tents, guns and ammunition, lamps, awls, pliers, chisels, adzes, handsaws, and hatchets. Presents for the Indians included such items as 4,600 assorted needles, 2,800 fishhooks, 12 pipe tomahawks, 48 calico ruffled shirts, ivory combs, yards of scarlet cloth, beads of all kinds, pocket mirrors, lockets, earrings, broaches, rings, knives, tobacco rolls, and a lot more.

1:00 P.M. I take notes in a different way than Bill does. I speak into my little tape recorder. I store my tapes in a waterproof case. When I get home, I'll listen to those tapes and type my journal out on paper. Bill works with a pen and small notebook. Sometimes he makes notes with one knee steadying the *Nikawa*'s jerky steering wheel. Every morning, before getting back on the river, Bill transfers his notes from the little notebook into a larger journal, or log, which he keeps in a black briefcase.

Lewis and Clark were among America's first travel writers. President Jefferson wanted each of them to keep a journal. If one man died, or if one journal got lost, then the other would be preserved. They kept their journals the way Bill does, with pen and paper. It must have been difficult for them to sit down and write after long days of illness and mosquitoes, hail and heat, hunger and exhaustion. Meriwether Lewis at one point wrote, "The ink freezes in my pen."

Although Lewis and Clark were the co-leaders of the expedition, their personalities were very different. Clark was a practical man of action. He was an even-tempered man. Lewis was more moody, more comfortable with abstract ideas. Yet there is not one record in their journals of a quarrel or fight between them. I know enough about journeys to say that there must have been times of tension. Traveling with friends can be difficult.

Profile portraits of Meriwether Lewis, *above left,* and William Clark, *right,* from *Original Journals of the Lewis and Clark Expedition,* ed. Reuben Thwaites, 1905. Missouri Historical Society

I hope Bill and I can get along well for a month. We are very different. Bill is a short, slender man with a grey beard and neatly combed grey hair. He is extremely orderly. I am tall, balding, and quite sloppy. Like all good captains, Bill runs a tight ship. Everything on Bill's boat has its proper place. He does not like it when I drop potato chips on the *Nikawa's* cabin floor.

In a way, Bill and I are getting to know each other for the first time. I've heard Bill has a powerful temper. I've heard he can go ballistic when things are not going just right. There's great pressure on him now, during the flood. Many things could go wrong. I just hope he doesn't yell at me. I hate to be yelled at.

The author takes the helm.

1:15 P.M. Bill lets me take the helm. The little steering wheel of the *Nikawa* is difficult to turn. It jolts out of my hands when we hit the boils—bubbling whirlpoollike things. The boils well up from the river with great force. Some are bigger than the *Nikawa.*

Looking at the riverbanks, we notice a change in the land. There's a touch of the Great Plains now.

Bill says, "See what Lewis and Clark say about this area."

So I take out my copy of the Lewis and Clark journals and read aloud.

July 30, 1804
This prairie is covered with grass of 10 or 12 inches in height, soil of good quality & at the distance of about a mile still further back the country rises about 80 or 90 feet higher, and is one continued plain as far as can be seen. The river meandering the open and beautiful plains. Catfish [are] caught in any part of the river. Turkeys, geese, and a beaver killed and caught. Everything in prime order. Men in high spirits.

The Channel

1:20 P.M. Bill and I are very different kinds of travelers. I like to get up early, leave early, and finish early, so I have the afternoon and evening to explore. Bill likes to get up late, have breakfast, and transfer his notes into his log. Often Bill won't get back on the river until noon or so. Then he travels into the evening. I will have to learn to travel on Bill's time.

In 1804, when Lewis and Clark moved up this lower part of the Missouri, the river was wide and shallow. It wandered across a wide plain, and was made up of several currents that crisscrossed each other like strands of hair in a braid.

Mile 641—Approaching DeSoto Bend

Trying to peg down the Missouri. Courtesy of U.S. Army Corps of Engineers

But now people have pegged this part of the river down. The current can no longer meander back and forth. On the lower Missouri, the U.S. Army Corps of Engineers has narrowed and deepened the channel. It has built levees, artificial banks that keep the river from moving from side to side. Now the river runs much faster.

During a flood (there have been six major floods since 1951), these levees sometimes cannot hold back the angry river. The water tops the levees and spreads into the towns and farms, like a trapped animal suddenly freed.

The lower 732 miles of the Missouri—from the Mississippi to Sioux City, Iowa—are called the *channelized river.* Here there are shipping lanes and buoys and markers for boats to follow. The lower Missouri has been so altered by the

The Missouri eats away at the riverbanks.

Corps that it's almost impossible to know where the river of Lewis and Clark actually ran. Even the length of the river has changed. Oxbows, great loops in the river, have been artificially straightened. The river has been shortened by more than a hundred miles.

Yet even the controlled river seems wild. No houses or condominiums clutter this shore. "The river would eat them alive," Bill says.

Now there are farms in the rich, low-lying areas within the floodplain—the land the river wants to flood into every spring. The farmers want protection against the floods. They say the Corps is not doing enough to control the river. They want even higher levees.

Environmentalists don't agree. They say the river would do less damage, not more, if it were allowed to flood normally. Certainly the wetlands and natural habitats for animals would return. Environmentalists also say that the limited commercial shipping is not worth the expense it takes to maintain this elaborate channel.

Today, there is not much river traffic. From 1820 through the 1880's, however, the Missouri River was full of steamboats. Trappers, gold miners, and homesteading pioneers traveled into the new land on paddle wheelers. But steamboats could not compete with the speedier, safer trains. The last steamboat left the upper Missouri in 1890. River towns faded into ghost towns. And now we can see the thousands of old wooden pilings everywhere along the shore, once used to control the river.

1:35 P.M. To avoid the underwater dikes (concrete posts used to trap sediment), we must stay in the channel. To help boats do this, the Corps has placed green and red markers on shore to show captains where to steer.

Our eyes strain to discover the markers as the *Nikawa* plows against the mad current. When I see the fluorescent green marker on the opposite shore, I say, "There it is!" Bill turns the wheel sharply, and we begin to cross the river, staying in the deeper channel.

Willow and cottonwood trees line the bank. Dark blue barn swallows, orange breasted with forked tails, flit from shore. They slice through the air, nearly touching the waves.

2:00 P.M. We come to DeSoto Bend, where the river once formed a loop many miles long. In 1959 the loop was separated from the river by dikes and levees. Cut off from the river, it became a lake, now a national wildlife refuge.

More than four hundred steamboats sank on the Missouri River. The 178-foot paddle wheeler *Bertrand* was one of them. In 1865 it hit a snag of tree trunks near DeSoto Bend, and sank in twelve feet of water. The river changed course over time and left the *Bertrand* in a field under thirty feet of silt and clay. The *Bertrand* was supposed to be carrying gold.

The Steamboat *Yellow Stone*, Karl Bodmer.
Joslyn Art Museum, Omaha, Nebraska

Treasure hunters searched for the boat for years, but it wasn't found until 1968. There was no gold. Like many of the steamers heading upriver in the 1860's, the *Bertrand* was carrying picks and shovels to open up new mines in Montana, hammers and saws to build towns, and plows and scythes to farm the new land. These artifacts are now in a museum, showing us what life on the frontier was like.

4:00 P.M. We pass a power plant, a concrete fortress without windows.

Bill says, "*Something's* going to get us!"

"What do you mean?"

Bill says that at the end of the day, just when he thinks he's home free—that's when something bad happens.

Idle work boats on the river today

4:15 P.M. Here the river is about a quarter of a mile wide. I'm surprised that we haven't seen any tugs or barges actually moving up or down the river. The few we've seen have been idle, tied up on shore. Bill says he hasn't seen a canoe in more than a month of travel from New York City. *Not one canoe.*

Today the Missouri, like the Mississippi, is measured from its highest pond source. The highest contributing waters for the Missouri are a couple of little lakes called Upper Red Rock Lake and Lower Red Rock, in Montana. The total length of the Missouri is 2,540 miles, a few hundred miles longer than the Mississippi. (If you combine the Missouri with the lower half of the Mississippi, you get the third longest river in the world, after the Amazon and the Nile.)

Bill says, "Lewis and Clark thought the river's highest contributing water was a little spring up on the Lemhi Pass, right on the Continental Divide. They weren't off by much." Bill admires the geographical skills of those early voyagers. "I'm amazed that they got as close as they did," he says, eyeing the river for drift.

Beaver. © Animals Animals

5:00 P.M. There's beaver sign on shore—downed trees with pointed ends where busy teeth have been working. Farmers don't like beavers because they dig into the levees. From the 1600's until the 1840's, however, the pelt of the beaver was considered "fur gold." Europeans demanded beaver pelts for their hats, and so trappers wandered the West in search of the "golden pelt."

Bill makes notes in his notebook while I hold the wheel for him. A blue heron takes flight from shore. Bill says, "Some believe that herons are the souls of river pilots."

Great blue heron. © Susan Van Etten

6:30 P.M. We are nearing Sioux City. The powerful smell of sewage begins as we approach civilization. Bill offers the wheel to me again. No sooner do I take the helm than we hit something. I cut the engines way back, and we check the props. Once again, we're lucky. Everything's okay.

Ahead I can see the Sergeant Floyd monument. The white shaft rises high above the trees on the east bank. It is a true Egyptian obelisk, a hundred feet tall. The monument was built in honor of Sergeant Floyd, the only member of the Lewis and Clark expedition to die *en route*. He probably had appendicitis.

13

Monday, August 20, 1804
Sergeant Floyd as bad as he can be, no pulse, and noth-
ing will stay a moment in his stomach . . . Sergeant Floyd
died with a great deal of composure. Before his death he
said to me, "I am going away. I want you to write me a
letter." We buried him on the top of the bluff a half mile
below a small river to which we gave his name.

Every year on the Saturday closest to August 20, the people of Sioux City trek up to the monument and shoot off a
salute in honor of Sergeant Floyd.

6:45 P.M. Bill calls on the shortwave radio: "*Nikawa* to
Bronco. *Nikawa* to Bronco. Do you read me?"

After a slight pause, Bob Lindholm's voice comes in
loud and clear. "Bronco to *Nikawa*, I read you."

We moor at the marina. And here are Bob and Scott, our
two other mates for the rest of the Missouri River. It's good to
see them. Bob is a tall bear of a man with white hair and a
thick white beard. He is good-natured and bright-eyed. He's a
retired lawyer from Jefferson City, Missouri. Scott Buchanan
is an old friend of Bill's from graduate school days. He's a
professor of English at a college in Kansas City, a fun-loving,
deep-voiced philosopher.

8:30 P.M. We joke and eat steaks at a local restaurant. With
lifted glasses, Bill toasts our journey: "Here's to one more day
on the river." Above Sioux City, the real nature of the Missouri
is about to show itself. Bill says to us, "Well, men, it's been a
piece of cake until now."

The Natural River

May 29 Memorial Day, 9:00 A.M. The day is bright, the sky deep blue. The air is crisp and clear as glass. A good omen, I hope.

This morning I call home. Walker is not in a good mood. He says, "Come home, Dad." I try to explain, "In one month, Walker." At two years old, my son has no idea how long a month is. He screams, "NO. COME HOME NOW." Then he hangs up the phone. When I call back, he refuses to speak to me.

Our destination, seventy-four miles upriver, is the dam at Yankton, the first of six major flood-control dams on the Missouri. Because of the flooding on the lower Missouri, the Corps of Engineers is holding back water in all the dams to protect the big cities on the lower river. With very little water coming out, the sections of river just below the dams are extremely shallow and will be our toughest going.

Bill and Scott speak to Strode Hinds.

10:00 A.M. Strode Hinds, a retired dentist in Sioux City, is an expert on Lewis and Clark. He has come down to meet us. He pulls out a book and says, "Let me read you something.

15

The Bronco driver and captain of the Nikawa plan checkpoints and destinations.

The Missouri *'cuts corners, runs around at night, lunches on levees, and swallows islands and small villages for dessert. It makes farming as fascinating as gambling. You never know whether you're going to harvest corn or catfish.'*

Strode laughs. He asks, "You have a depth finder on that boat? Good. You'll learn when you get upstream that there are all kinds of little riffles and currents. Just watch out if you see any real disturbance on the water. It means there's something darn close to the surface! And be ready to push, drag, or pole yourself off a bar! That's how Lewis and Clark got up here. Doing a lot of poling."

Scott, Bob, and I are the designated drivers of the Bronco. Whoever drives the Bronco is the sole support for the expedition. We have many dams and waterfalls ahead of us. We cannot get around them without the trailer. If the car gets into an accident, Bill's trip will fail. I will begin the driving today. Then I'll have two days on the river while Bob and Scott each take a day driving.

Our two-way radio has a five-mile range. Bill says it only

works well over flat water. If there's a hill in the way, forget it. Getting within five miles of the boat will be difficult. Roads don't always follow rivers. Therefore, we also arrange checkpoints, places to meet during the day's run. Today, we've agreed to meet at Ponca.

10:30 A.M. Bill has finished transcribing yesterday's notes into his journal. The *Nikawa* motors slowly out of the marina and quickly disappears around the first river bend. I leap into the Bronco and head out. It's my first time driving such a big vehicle dragging a large trailer.

But driving the Bronco, I discover, is fun. It breaks up the monotony of river travel and gives me a chance to see the river from the land. On their voyage, Lewis and Clark struck a nice balance of water *and* land travel. Lewis himself often walked along shore while Clark stayed with the boats. The men who hunted for the expedition's food left the boats in the morning and rejoined the expedition in the evening.

12:00 P.M. The road runs through wide, open rolling hills dotted with cattle. In Nebraska everyone waves at everyone else, so I wave at the cars I pass. Western meadowlarks sing on fence posts.

Mile 762—Ponca, Nebraska

In the little farming village of Ponca, the *Nikawa* shows up just when I get to the boat ramp. We drivers learn quickly that traveling by road often takes twice as long as it does by river. We Bronco busters have to drive like crazy to keep up with the boat. In fact, driving the Bronco is often harder work than traveling in the *Nikawa*.

Lewis and Clark killed their first buffalo near Ponca. Like the musk ox of the arctic tundra, buffalo are an ancient animal that survived the ice ages in North America.

Thursday, August 24, 1804
J. Fields sent out to hunt. Came to the boat and informed that he had killed a buffalo in the plain ahead. Capt. Lewis took 12 men and had the buffalo brought to the boat in the next bend. Two elk swam the river and [were] fired at from the boat. Several prairie wolves [coyotes] seen today. Saw elk standing on a sandbar.

Slaughtered for the hide: buffalo skinners on the Great Plains: colored engraving, 1874. THE GRANGER COLLECTION

As the prairie was settled, the big game disappeared. Elk and grizzlies retreated westward to the mountains. Buffalo were slaughtered—sixty million of them—mainly for their hides. A buffalo hunter could kill two hundred buffalo a day with a long-range, high-powered rifle.

Sometimes buffalo were killed merely for political reasons. People knew the Plains Indians depended on the buffalo. When the buffalo were gone, the Indians could be defeated and controlled.

The buffalo are no longer endangered. On a few isolated ranches, they are raised for meat. Some buffalo herds now roam the national parks. But what would sixty million buffalo look like?

Mile 792—Sportsman's Restaurant

2:30 P.M. The *Nikawa* is late. Something's wrong. *Ckscksckscks.* Nothing but static on the radio. Every ten minutes I try to raise Bill on the shortwave. "Bronco to *Nikawa*, Bronco to *Nikawa*. Do you read me, over." *Cksckscksck.*

Power boats zoom by the shore near the restaurant. Water-skiers zip past. Across the river on an island, a herd of cattle wade into the cool water. Cornstalks float downstream at five miles an hour. Scott and I have found a river guide named Billy Joe Conrad. He is a heavyset man wearing a blue-checked shirt, blue jeans, and a white baseball cap.

Billy Joe and his friends are angry at the Corps of Engineers. The Corps constantly raises and lowers the level of the water. It is trying to save endangered piping plovers and least terns by keeping them from nesting on the sandbars. Billy Joe says the walleye fishing has been terrible ever since the Corps started this policy. He says it's just another example of messing with Mother Nature.

Billy Joe shakes his head in anger. Then he hops in a friend's boat and heads downriver. He promises to keep an eye out for the *Nikawa*.

Above, Endangered piping plover; *below,* least tern. Courtesy of Dr. John Ferrell, U.S. Army Corps of Engineers

4:00 P.M. Finally the *Nikawa* comes into sight. Billy Joe is aboard. Billy Joe found them stranded on a sandbar. They pushed and poled until they were free.

Wonderful news! Billy Joe has agreed to guide the *Nikawa* up to the dam. Bill asks me if I want to come. "Peter, you should see this section of the river," he says.

4:25 P.M. How time slows down when you're nervous! We're crossing the river between sandbars running from one bank to the other, zigzagging our way up to the dam. Billy Joe, raising his hand, says, "Okay, go right."

While Bill and I stare tensely at the water, waiting any

moment to hit a sandbar, Billy Joe looks as cool as an astronaut. "Now left," he says calmly. Bill then swings the *Nikawa* hard to port.

The river widens. The sandbars multiply. We pass islands, too. Some are three miles long. Here, finally, is the braided river, much as Lewis and Clark would have seen it.

"Always look ahead," Billy Joe warns us. "See that ripple way up there. See it?" I strain to see something, but it all looks the same—just a glare of water. I wonder how Lewis and Clark managed without sunglasses! Two years of river glare must have turned their eyes to leather.

"That's a bar," Billy Joe says. "Now cut right, hard right."

Bill drops the speed of the engines a bit, and Billy Joe shouts, "No, no. Keep her going. Keep her on top. You'll draw less water."

5:15 P.M. Billy Joe suddenly says "stop." And we float in the current. We can see the city of Yankton, South Dakota. Billy Joe says, "Logs or rocks?"

"What?"

He explains: There are rocks on one side of the river and deadheads on the other. A deadhead is an invisible, submerged tree stump sticking up from the bottom of the river. Deadheads can break motors beyond repair. So can rocks!

Bill chooses deadheads. "I'd rather hit a log than a rock," he says. And we pick our way slowly through an invisible minefield of submerged trees. At Yankton, the banks of the river are supported with old cars. People will build up the levees with anything they find.

Building the riverbanks with junk

In a place called Box Car Bend, whole boxcars were thrown into the river to keep the water from washing away the railroad tracks.

5:45 P.M. We have reached the dam, a massive concrete wall blocking the river ahead. Scott and Bob are here to meet us.

Lewis and Clark set aside three hundred dollars for paying hunters, guides, and interpreters. What could we pay Billy Joe for getting us through the sandbars? Nothing. He's just glad to help out.

8:00 P.M. We have dinner at the marina. We feel like a real team now. Bill says, "Here's to surviving another darn day on the river."

CHAPTER FOUR

Lake or River?

May 30, 1995, 9:00 A.M. The *Nikawa* sits on its trailer in the marina parking lot above the dam. At breakfast in a small diner, Bill takes a booth by himself for an hour. He transcribes yesterday's notes.

Gavin's Point Dam at Yankton produces hydroelectric power and controls water flow down to St. Louis. The twenty-five-mile lake that formed on the upriver side of the dam is called Lewis and Clark Lake. The lake has the highest water level it's had in twenty years. We are told that marinas and boat ramps upriver are flooded. Getting the *Nikawa* in and out might be difficult. We are warned about the winds, too. High winds can whip up storms out of nowhere and swamp small craft like the *Nikawa*.

In 1944 Congress passed a law to build six dams on the Missouri River. The lakes formed by these dams line up for more than one thousand miles. Some call these lakes the "Great Lakes of the Missouri." They have flooded thousands of acres of river valley. Many Indian villages, battlefields, fur trading posts, and hundreds of Lewis and Clark sites now lie under water.

12:00 P.M. Getting around the dams depends on good boat ramps and teamwork. First, the Bronco driver backs the trailer into the water on the concrete ramp below the dam. Bill, at the *Nikawa's* helm, approaches slowly. Nosing the bow of the boat onto the end of the trailer, he guns the engines. The *Nikawa* actually seems to climb out of the water onto the rollers of the trailer. This is particularly difficult in any kind of wind or current.

Mile 806—Gavin's Point Dam, Yankton, South Dakota

On facing page, The dam at Yankton; *below,* Teamwork

Launching the *Nikawa* into Lewis and Clark Lake

After the *Nikawa* runs as far as it can onto the rollers of the submerged trailer, we attach a wire cable from the trailer's winch to the eye hook on the *Nikawa's* bow. The boat is then slowly winched into position on the trailer, and is dragged out of the water dripping and glistening in the sun.

This takes time. Today we are reversing the process, and launching the boat into Lewis and Clark Lake on the upriver side of the dam. We're all learning how to do this.

The visitor's center at the dam is very near the location where Lewis and Clark met their first Sioux. Contact with the Sioux was one of the expedition's main objectives, because the Sioux had all but closed the river to traders. On August 29, 1804, Lewis and Clark met with five chiefs and seventy warriors of the Yankton Sioux.

Clark wrote many pages in his journal about the customs, language, tribal divisions, names, and beliefs of the Sioux. He wrote: "This great nation, who the French has given the nickname of Sioux, call themselves Dakota [meaning friends or allies]."

August 29, 1804

The lodges of the Sioux are of a conical form, covered with buffalo robes painted with various figures and colors, with a hole in the top for the smoke to pass through. The lodges contain from 10 to 15 persons. The interior arrangement is compact and handsome.

August 30, 1804

The Sioux are a stout, bold-looking people, the young men handsome and well made. The greater part of them make use of bows and arrows. The warriors are very much decorated with paint, porcupine quills and feathers, large leggings, and moccasins—all with buffalo robes of different colors. The squaws wore petticoats and . . . white buffalo robe[s] with the black hair turned back over their necks and shoulders. In the evening the whole party danced until a late hour.

Sioux Indians at ball play on the ice: engraving, 1855 after a drawing by Seth Eastman. THE GRANGER COLLECTION

1:00 P.M. Another postcard-perfect day—it's sunny and 78 degrees. The sky is dotted with clouds. Along the far shore of the lake the high bluffs are layered in dark and white lines made from shale, chalk, and limestone. The Great Plains leading down to the western shore are pastel green.

We'll run up to the town of Niobrara in the *Nikawa*. Locals tell us the water is very low. In fact, we're not sure we can make it. Maybe we'll have to switch to the canoe. Or perhaps we'll have to drag the canoe by ropes. I'm all for it. Bill says, smiling, "Pete, you're just dying to do what Lewis and Clark did, aren't you?"

"You bet," I fire back. "To heck with motors!" Secretly, of course, I'm glad we have engines. To fight the Missouri current here by paddling a canoe would be madness.

Trying to find the channel

2:00 P.M. Today we pay close attention to our depth finder. But it doesn't work so well when the boat bounces around. On our charts many sections are labeled, "Submerged Trees." The natural channel, the one Lewis and Clark and the steamboats followed, is buried now. So are the old islands. But the river's channel is still changing—even now when it's buried beneath so much water. Such is the power of this river.

The shallowness at the far end of the lake worries Bill. But we agree the only way to tackle the journey is to take each day, each hour, as it comes along. One thing at a time. That's the way Lewis and Clark must have tackled their expedition, one day, one problem at a time.

4:00 P.M. We're stumped. We can't travel any farther than the town of Niobrara. It's just too shallow from here to our second dam, the Fort Randall Dam. The next thirty-seven miles are full of snags and bars. We're going to pull out and drive around this section. Bill might come back later and run downstream, just to say he covered this section by water.

Where the river has flooded the bank and left backwater pools, a boy holding a pitchfork is spearfishing buffalo, a bottom-feeding fish of the sucker family. The boy's father says buffalo are bony eating. "Since the river got dammed," he says, "the town of Niobrara has been flooded out twice. Each time, we move back from the river. In 1976, the last time we moved, the population of Niobrara dropped from seven hundred to four hundred. It's depressing."

A boy spearfishing

Taking the *Nikawa* out of the river is not easy. The ramp is blocked by a huge tree trunk. Bob and I put a chain around the tree and drag it to one side with the Bronco.

5:30 P.M. I feel the land getting wilder. There's a wonderful free feeling out here on the prairie. We're entering ranch country, the high plains. The upper Missouri begins here.

On our drive around this impossible stretch of river, I encourage Bill to make a detour into Ponca State Park. I want a panoramic view of the Niobrara River, which feeds into the

Missouri from western Nebraska. The Niobrara is the first of many great tributaries coming mostly from the west. Each one has its own history. Some day I'll return to explore the great tributaries of the Missouri—the Kansas, the Platte, the Cheyenne, the Grand, and the Yellowstone rivers. I've been told the Niobrara is great for canoeing!

Bill is reluctant to drive on the narrow and steep park road while dragging a three thousand pound boat. He says sharply, "If we get stuck in here, Pete, there might be a court-martial." It's a running joke. Every time one of us crew members makes a mistake, Bill threatens to court-martial us. Bill was in the U.S. Navy.

From the top of a high hill we can see where the *Nikawa* came today. A long sandbar forms directly across the whole river. Bill is perplexed. He says, "What makes a sandbar go *across* the current! How can that happen? Down in my part of the river, the bars form *with* the current!" This is yet another example of the wackiness of the river. We can also see clearly the wide and braided Niobrara as it feeds into the Missouri from the west, adding tons and tons of silt. No wonder we can't run this section.

When the four of us squeeze once more into the Bronco, I look back at our wonderful boat, now perched on its trailer. I can't help feeling that the *Nikawa* is like a loyal dog following in our footsteps.

We can smell the strong fumes from our extra gas tanks. I ask Bill, "So how does it feel to be driving along the river instead of running it?" He says with a laugh like bullet fire, "A relief!" I detect a certain regret in his voice, too.

Along the western shore we pass over soft rolling hills. In tiny farming communities the pungent smell of hog farms is stronger than the gasoline fumes.

May 30, 7:00 P.M. Dusk settles over the plains as we drive into Fort Randall. The foundations of the original fort are still visible just below the dam. Built in 1856, the fort was the first in a chain of forts on the upper Missouri River. Soldiers here provided military protection to settlers up and down the river. They escorted wagon trains across the plains. They battled with Sioux warriors.

Chief Sitting Bull, a powerful medicine man and leader of the Sioux, was once held prisoner at Fort Randall. He and his band of Hunkpapa Sioux made camp outside the fort. For two years, hundreds of people came to see the famous chief. Then he was moved to another fort.

Fort Randall Casino

Sioux guards at the Fort Randall Casino

7:30 P.M. We drive a few miles to the east and discover the Fort Randall Casino-Hotel high on a hill in the empty South Dakota prairie. Neon signs outside the casino flash: "Restaurant: All You Can Eat . . . Open 24 Hours . . ." The parking lot is full of cars and buses. I wonder where all the people come from. The building itself is made of grey planks to imitate a fort.

The Sioux, like many reservation Indians today, have found a much-needed source of income in gambling casinos. Often reservations are isolated, far away from big cities—and from jobs. In states where gambling is otherwise illegal, the government has allowed Indians to build and run casinos on reservation land. This helps generate money for tribal programs.

Here, we find many Yankton Sioux guards walking around the casino, hotel, and restaurant, making sure there is no trouble. In dark blue police uniforms, they are tall, big-shouldered men with jet black hair. Their faces are somber and handsome.

The Yankton Sioux at Fort Randall number about 2,500. One Sioux woman tells me that since she was a child, the reservation has grown much stronger. The casino has been profitable. Jobs are more numerous. The tribe is even building a new truck stop across the road. The Dakota language is being taught to the children on the reservation. Many of her people still swim and fish in the river, where there are bald and golden eagles.

The Teton Sioux

May 31, 9:00 A.M. We drive the *Nikawa* down the hill into Pickstown, South Dakota to get fuel for the boat. First we pump gas into the two large tanks built into the sides of the boat; then we fill five, six-gallon

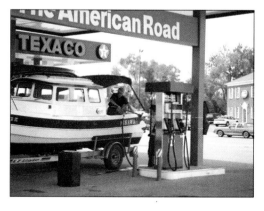

Bill fills the tanks.

Mile 880—Pickstown, South Dakota

plastic canisters for extra fuel. The odd sight of the *Nikawa* at the gas pump gets a lot of comments.

2:00 P.M. After so much rain, we're fortunate the good weather is holding. We study the charts and the landforms ahead. The wind is brisk out of the southwest, the chop moderate.

Mile 921—on Lake Francis Case

We head mostly north, out over the wide lake. Treeless hills roll down to the western shore. The sky is a soft grey. We've seen mergansers, grebes, cormorants, and muskrats.

Floating trees are everywhere! Scott and I take turns up front with Bill, eyeing the lake for the deadly logs. We pass a particularly big one—maybe three times longer than the *Nikawa*. Often they lie hidden in the troughs between the waves. When a log gets sloshed around in a lake for weeks or even months, it absorbs water. It sinks deeper and deeper below the surface. We call these "low riders." Hitting a low rider today might strand us in the middle of nowhere. These lakes are remote. In fact, from here on up to Fort Peck is some of the most isolated, empty land in the country.

31

Mile 967—Chamberlain, South Dakota

5:00 P.M. We dock in Chamberlain, South Dakota, for the night. The marina parking lot is flooded. A wall of sandbags surrounds a cafe. The cafe looks as if it's floating. A boy on top of the sand bags is bow fishing. We tie the *Nikawa* securely to the floating dock, but there is no way for us to walk to the Bronco without rolling up our pants and carrying our gear, hip-deep in water. We laugh as Bill unzips the lower half of his long pants, and voila! he's in shorts!

Sandbagging on the Missouri River

June 1, 1:00 P.M. Today, I'm in the Bronco. I back the trailer into the water at our third dam, Big Bend Dam, and deposit the *Nikawa* into eighty-mile-long Lake Sharpe.

The road to the capital city of Pierre (pronounced "peer") runs along a tabletop of prairie, high above the lake, high above the river. From the prairie the river is invisible because it has cut a deep path for itself.

The few cars and pickup trucks I pass are driven by men in cowboy hats. At one point, I spot the *Nikawa* far below, a

tiny speck in a sea of sky and water. Along much of the banks, dead trees stick out of the lake like a ghost forest. There is little wildlife.

In 1804 Lewis and Clark were the first to write about pronghorn antelope, mule deer, cutthroat trout, the western meadowlark, grizzly bear, the pack rat, and the black-tailed prairie dog.

On September 17, 1804, Meriwether Lewis, tired of traveling on the boat, headed inland with six of his best hunters. They came across villages of barking squirrels [prairie dogs] and pronghorn antelope, which he called "goats." Lewis was impressed with the pronghorn's shy and watchful nature, with its agility and speed. (Pronghorn can sprint up to sixty miles an hour!)

Tuesday, September 18, 1804
The hunters killed 10 deer today and a prairie wolf [coyote]. Had it all jerked and skins stretched after camping. I walked on shore, saw goats [pronghorn antelope], elk, buffalo, black tail deer, and the common deer. I killed a prairie wolf, about the size of a grey fox . . . The large wolves [grey wolf] are very numerous.

North American elk. © John Reddy

Mile 1,064—Pierre, South Dakota

5:00 P.M. In Pierre, I hear Bob on the radio long before the *Nikawa* reaches the capital, where the Teton (or Bad) River feeds into the Missouri. Pierre is a small city with wide sandy beaches. Children swim and fish right downtown. Zip-sleds buzz in the late afternoon. Pontoon boats run back onto the beaches, and families have cookouts within sight of the capital building. I guide the *Nikawa* into the marina.

The sky is on fire. The puffy clouds turn a flaming orange. Bill says, "There's nothing like the Great Plains for skies!"

All of us are tired now. We four are thrown together much of the day and night. It's tiring to be with the same people all the time. Traveling all day in the hot glare of a river puts you outside normal time. There is nothing but the waves and the wind and the open sky. It is easy to forget the world and its problems. Our daily task is simply to move ahead, always ahead. When I get home from my river trips, friends often ask me, "Well, was it fun?" And I have to tell them, yes, but there were many moments when it was no fun at all.

Bill and I speak occasionally about travel writing. Bill says

It's the people that make a river interesting.

the word travel comes from the word "travail," meaning painful, heavy work. Bill says he likes to look at his photographs after a long, hard journey. Remembering a trip from his home, he feels a kind of bliss, even though he's bone tired.

Scott likes nothing better than to chat with river rats, people who live on the water. Scott has confided to me that he's frustrated we're moving upriver so fast. He says, "It seems pretty senseless, just getting in a boat and watching the water. It's the *people* that make a river interesting." He wants us to slow down, but we cannot.

As Lewis and Clark approached present day Pierre near-ly two hundred years ago, they grew tense. They expected trouble from the Teton Sioux, who were the strongest of all the Sioux groups.

George Catlin, "Bear Dance, Sioux preparing for a bear hunt." Gilcrease Museum, Tulsa, Oklahoma

Hundreds of Tetons gathered along the river. They could easily have massacred the explorers, but did not, perhaps because of the bravery and determination shown by Clark and his men. Once during the encounter, the Teton warriors strung their bows and drew arrows from their quivers as if to shoot. Lewis then ordered his men to point their rifles at the chiefs. Suddenly Black Buffalo, the grand chief, put a stop to the intimidation, and a fight was avoided.

On September 26 both Clark and Lewis were carried on white buffalo robes to the great council lodge in the Teton village. Buffalo meat was roasted over fires. Speeches were made by Black Buffalo and the explorers, but no competent interpreter was present. No one was certain what the other was saying. Most likely the chief was demanding that the explorers trade only with the Sioux. Black Buffalo raised a sacred pipe and made a prayer. He smoked and passed the pipe in a circle for all to smoke. The explorers were offered dog meat (a delicacy to the Tetons). Musicians played tambourines, shook rattles, and sang. Teton women danced with the scalps of slain enemies.

Again, fearing an attack at any time, Clark slept little. "I am very unwell for want of sleep," he wrote.

Two days later the boats moved upriver once again. But Lewis and Clark had not accomplished Jefferson's goal of making a friendly impression on the Sioux.

9:00 P.M. We drive through Pierre, a charming city. We stop for soft ice-cream cones. Bill tells me a story.

By the early 1700's, the French fur trade stretched clear across the continent from Quebec, Canada, to the Rocky Mountains. That is why there are a lot of French names, like Pierre, along the upper Missouri. In 1743, a French fur-trader buried a small lead plate, eight inches long, in the hills near present-day Pierre. The plate claimed the land for the king of France.

In 1913 three teenagers were walking in the hills. One of them kicked a grey object with her boot. And voila! They had found the lead tablet buried so long before. On it was a Latin inscription, which is still readable today. The words claimed the land for "our most illustrious sovereign, Louis XV." The tablet is now on display in a museum in Pierre.

Sitting Bull

June 2, 12:00 P.M. Just north of Pierre, we take the *Nikawa* around Oahe Dam, the ninth largest dam in the world. We then set off on Lake Oahe. The biggest lake in the Missouri River system, it stretches 231 miles, from the capital of South Dakota to Bismarck, the capital of North Dakota.

Mile 1,069—Oahe Dam

To give Bill a rest, I take the helm for a spell. Bob navigates. We all watch closely for drifting logs. I'm mesmerized by sun and sky and glare. Franklin's gulls, white with black heads and black wing tips, soar above us, laughing and crying. Never before has the Missouri looked more like an ocean. For a long while we can't even see the shore. I'd hate to be caught out in the middle of this lake in a canoe.

When the dams were built, islands submerged in the river.

Lewis and Clark came to this place on October 1, 1804. Because they expected a fight with the Sioux, they named an island here, the Island of Caution.

We motor right over the Island of Caution in the *Nikawa*. We see it first on our charts, then we see the depth finder change suddenly to much shallower numbers. The Island of Caution is one of the many Lewis and Clark sites drowned by the reservoir system.

1:30 P.M. Lake Oahe has more than 2,250 miles of shoreline. Bill motors to shore. We tie the bow and stern lines to bushes and climb a hill. The wind blows hard across the prairie. Lovely wind, eternal wind. How remote this place seems. We eat peanut butter and jelly sandwiches and look down at the *Nikawa* bobbing gently back and forth against the bank.

Mile 1,195—Standing Rock Indian Reservation

6:30 P.M. We pull into a marina on the Standing Rock Reservation. We dock on a spit of land, where the Grand River joins the lake. (It is hard to call this huge Lake Oahe the Missouri River, but it is.) We have come 131 miles today. This is one of the longest one-day distances Bill has racked up on his entire trip.

Nearby we see large white canvas tipis. Sioux children have come for a weekend retreat, to camp, swim, fish, and canoe.

Two Oglala Sioux boys

While we go about the business of securing the *Nikawa* for the night, we chat with two boys who are swimming apart from their friends. They laugh and show us their muscles. Jason and Seth are Oglala Sioux. They say they understand the Lakota language but don't speak it. Their parents and grandparents still speak Lakota.

The great Hunkpapa Sioux chief Sitting Bull was born on the Grand River a few miles west of where we are docking the *Nikawa* for the night. And he died here, on the Standing Rock Reservation.

40

As a child Sitting Bull was called Slow because he was deliberate in his actions. He studied things before he acted. From an early age he showed signs of leadership. At ten he received his first pony and killed his first buffalo. At fourteen he became a warrior, and his name was changed from Slow to Sitting Bull. By that time the first wagon trains were beginning to cross the Great Plains, heading for Oregon.

The U.S. government had agreed in 1868 to stay off Indian land, west of the Missouri River. But in 1874 came the

Sitting Bull. The Library of Congress.

discovery of gold in the Black Hills. Prospectors invaded Sioux land. At first, the U.S. government kept the gold diggers out. Then, it tried to convince the Sioux to sell the Black Hills, which were sacred.

Sitting Bull had watched soldiers rounding up tribes all around him, forcing them onto reservations. Now, if they tried to take the Black Hills, he was determined to fight. He told his people, "We are an island of Indians in a lake of whites. We must stand together, or they will wipe us out separately. The white soldiers have come shooting. They want war. All right, we'll give it to them."

Then he sent for warriors from all the fighting tribes west of the Missouri River: the Cheyenne, the Blackfeet, the Arapaho, and the Sioux. It was the first—and last—time ever that thousands of Plains Indians would fight as one.

On June 25, 1876, General George Custer attacked Sitting

Bull. Custer wanted glory, and thought he was attacking only a few hundred Indians. Thousands of Indians from all the tribes counterattacked. Custer's two hundred soldiers were wiped out in the Battle of Little Big Horn, often called "Custer's Last Stand."

Winning one small battle could not save the Indians. Exhaustion, starvation, and superior military force soon drove the Sioux out of their sacred Black Hills. The buffalo were gone, and the fierce Teton Sioux were forced onto reservations, including the Standing Rock Reservation.

Sioux Indians breaking up camp, Seth Eastman circa 1848, oil on canvas. THE GRANGER COLLECTION

43

6:45 P.M. We leave the boys and the *Nikawa*, and jump into the Bronco. We drive to the little town of Mobridge—a poor town with a few hotels and restaurants and bars. Residents call Mobridge the "Walleye Capital of the World." We find lots of fisherman in Mobridge. One fisherman asks, "Where you boys headed? All the way to Bismarck?"

"No," Scott says, "we're going to the Pacific Ocean!" The man laughs. Perhaps he thinks we're a little crazy.

8:00 P.M. An Indian wedding party celebrates in the back room of a dark, smoky restaurant. We can see the wonderful faces of the old women and the old men—classic weather-beaten Indian faces. Some of the men wear long black braids and bright colorful shirts.

When we leave the restaurant Bill whispers, "You know, Pete, that could be Sitting Bull's relatives in there."

June 3, 10:00 A.M. I have only an hour to find Sitting Bull's grave. I drive onto the reservation, and finally discover a small dirt track off a paved road. Around the monument, there are no cars, no tourists. Some cattle are grazing in a nearby field.

Sitting Bull's grave sits high on a bluff, not far from his birthplace on the Grand River. Here the remains of the dead chief are embedded in twenty tons of concrete. On the solid block of concrete is a bust of Sitting Bull. It is a round, handsome, wise face that gazes at the Missouri River.

After the Battle of Little Big Horn, Sitting Bull went north into Canada for safety. Then he gave himself up. He returned to a small cabin on the Grand River. He was critical of corrupt government agents who stole reservation money and supplies. In 1890 Indian police working for one of these agents shot and killed Sitting Bull.

For sixty years his grave was neglected. Then on a dark, cold, and raw spring night in 1953, a group of his relatives dug up his remains and reburied them high on this bluff overlooking Lake Oahe.

On the monument I find his Indian name: "Tatanka Iyotake: Sitting Bull (1831-1890)."

The location is so beautiful, so full of sadness. I say into the wind: "I pray you did not die in vain, Tatanka Iyotake. I pray for you, Sitting Bull, and for your people."

The grave of Sitting Bull overlooking the river

PART THREE

North Dakota

CHAPTER SEVEN

Trouble

June 3, 1:00 P.M. It is a gorgeous afternoon. Even so, I have a strong sense that something is about to go wrong. I can't shake the feeling.

It's good weather, yes, but with very strong winds, huge waves, and lots of pounding and battered nerves. The drift is dangerous. Scott shakes his head. Looking frustrated he says, "We have to fight the drift and all the waves, just to stay on the river."

Checking the motors for snags

Today we cross over the border into North Dakota. Ninety percent of North Dakota is farmland. Lewis and Clark spent more than two hundred days here. Our checkpoint is at Fort Yates.

Buttes and mesas and cone-shaped hills make this terrain feel more and more like the Wild West. Along the shore sagebrush is prevalent. Sagebrush is that blue, smoky-grey weed that dominates the West. What a smell! Wild and pungent.

Here Lewis and Clark encountered the Arikara people. They were farmers and lived in large earthen lodges.

Friday, October 12, 1804
[The Arikara] live in warm houses, large and built in an octagon form, forming a cone at top, which is left open for the smoke to pass. Those houses are generally 30 or 40 foot [in] diameter, covered with earth on poles, willows, and grass to prevent the earth passing through.

On facing page: Mandan, North Dakota.
© John Elk, III/Stock Boston.

Mile 1,248—Fort Yates

Scott and Hunkpapa Sioux family at Fort Yates

4:00 P.M. Bob is the Bronco buster today. He drives as fast as he can to beat the *Nikawa* to Fort Yates. But he barely arrives in time to meet us. The wind makes docking extremely dangerous. Bill is irritable at moments like this. Today Bob is the object of Bill's anger. Rather than helping guide the *Nikawa*, Bob is busy taking pictures of us as we come into the dock. Bill is furious. "Put that camera down," Bill yells into the radio. "You've got a job to do!" Foremost of all our duties is to keep the *Nikawa* safe and running upriver.

In the cabin over the *Nikawa's* door, before he left home, Bill placed a large sign that says: Avoid Irritation. It must be a reminder to himself. On difficult days like today, we all get on each others' nerves.

When we finally dock safely, an Indian family comes over to have a look. Bill asks the father what his tribe is. The man says Sioux. "No," Bill says, "there are all kinds of Sioux. Which are you?" The man is startled. Most people don't make the distinction. He says proudly that he is Hunkpapa, "like Sitting Bull."

Mile 1,275—Fort Rice

White bass at Fort Rice

6:00 P.M. At the Fort Rice boat ramp, fishermen clean walleye pike and white bass on blood-soaked tables. The clear scales flash in the sunlight. One old fisherman says we sure picked the right time to come up the Missouri. The water is real-

48

ly high. But three years ago there was a drought. "You couldn't have made it then," he says.

He remembers the river before it became a lake. There were beautiful farms around here. Now those farms are all under water. I gaze out at thousands of half-submerged dead trees in the lake.

June 4, 11:00 A.M. This morning we have the "canoe debate." As the river gets shallower, we will have this debate all the way up into Montana. The canoe debate occurs whenever we get conflicting reports from river rats about how deep the river really is. Should we, or should we not, use the canoe? Even though it

The *Nikawa* keeping close to shore

makes him nervous, Bill usually opts for distance, and the only way to cover long distances is to use the *Nikawa*.

On shore I see magpies and Canada geese. Lilacs are in bloom. Clark reported frequent sightings of golden eagles or hawks. He saw a gang of buffalo bulls. His hunters killed four pronghorn antelope, six deer, four elk, and a white pelican.

2:00 P.M. Bill, Bob, and Scott had no problem with this morning's run to Mandan, a small city directly across the river from Bismarck. But the next ninety miles to the dam won't be so easy. The owner of the Broken Oar Marina, Scott Johnson, says we'll definitely need someone to guide us up to Washburn, where we hope to spend the night. Scott tells us an interesting story about Burnt Creek, which is just upriver.

Fur traders on the Missouri River attacked
by Indians: colored engraving, 1868.
THE GRANGER COLLECTION

In 1863 a group of twenty-one white men, one woman
and two children were returning in a small flatboat from the
goldfields of Montana. They had ninety thousand dollars
worth of gold dust aboard. They were advised not to travel
south because Sioux were camping along the Missouri. The
miners departed anyway. At the mouth of a small creek, an
Indian hailed the boat. The miners shot the man. The dead
Indian was from a nearby Sioux village. The boat got stranded on a sandbar, and the Indians from the village attacked.
They killed everyone aboard, at the cost of thirty-six Sioux
dead. All the gold dust was scattered on shore. When he heard

about the disaster, a trader employed two Indians to retrieve any gold dust they could find. The two men collected about seventy thousand dollars worth of dust from the riverbank. For payment the Indians were given one horse, a few trinkets, and a feast.

2:30 P.M. Two good-natured river rats with a speedboat have agreed to lead us partway to the next dam. So after another canoe debate, Bill decides to try the *Nikawa*. Bill's the captain, and he wants to make some distance. He won't change to the canoe yet.

The *Nikawa* follows the speedboat. I race the Bronco along the river roads. I've taken a second day Bronco busting because soon we'll be switching to the canoe. I want as much time in the canoe as I can get.

Leaving Mandan for the uncertain river

5:00 P.M. Fortunately, I just happen to be parked high on a bluff overlooking the river when the two boats come into view. I can see up and down the river for miles. It's a mess of sandbars with no clear way through. First I watch the speedboat turn around and head back toward Bismarck. Then the *Nikawa* moves forward slowly. From up here, a hundred feet above the river, I now see a possible channel. Bill's nowhere near it. I call on the radio. Bill will not go the way I suggest. Suddenly, the boat goes dead in the water. He's hit a rock. The call comes over the radio to find help. They're drifting downriver to what looks like a natural boat ramp. Bill calls sternly over the radio, "I'm coming out, no matter what."

I knock at the door of the ranch house across the road. The rancher, Arlen Simons, kindly agrees to help. He says this ranch has been in his family since 1872. He's got 1,300 acres of ranch land here. He and his son open a barbed-wire fence and lead me down a steep dirt track to the pebbly beach below. With difficulty, I back the trailer into the water.

One of the *Nikawa's* props is badly damaged. The boat putters to the trailer. When we try to pull the *Nikawa* out on the beach, the Bronco tires spin. So we strap another chain around Arlen's vehicle. Together, the two four-wheelers drag poor *Nikawa* out of the Missouri.

Behind the barn at the ranch, Bill replaces the broken prop. He says, "I should have listened to you, Pete. Tomorrow we can do it the Lewis and Clark way."

The Canoe at Last!

June 5, 11:30 A.M. Bill and I jump in the canoe. Bill takes the stern. Because it's our first day in the canoe, he wants to run the little Evinrude motor himself. I'm in the bow. Occasionally I duck, so he can see logs or sandbars ahead, and he swerves to avoid them. We move about five miles an hour against the current.

This certainly is beautiful terrain, wide open, with no people. Big old cottonwoods on shore. A few farms.

Mile 1,325—The Simons ranch, Wilton, North Dakota

Heading out in the canoe for the first time

Young Canada geese waddle along shore, scared of our motor, but unable yet to fly. The water is more green than brown. Swallows dip and swirl out of the high banks.

5:00 P.M. My first two white pelicans! Regal creatures, the big birds don't budge from their logs. They're too busy fishing. Lewis and Clark once shot a pelican to fill up its beak and see how much water it could hold. Five gallons!

Mile 1,355—Washburn, North Dakota

White pelicans. © R. & D. Aitenhead/Animals Animals

We double back and forth searching for the channel. We're like an ant struggling up this river. When we hit bottom, the motor bucks. But the little plastic prop keeps spinning. Hours pass slowly. My body goes numb. The aluminum seat is so hard I should sit on my life jacket, but I'm afraid to take it off. Bill is wise. He's brought a plastic seat to make these canoe days a little less hard on the body. Finally, we pull out at Washburn for the night.

7:00 P.M. Perhaps he's crazy, but Bill is thinking about trying the *Nikawa* again tomorrow, to save time. Once again, the canoe debate begins.

A local fisherman says, "You can make it. Heck, yes." He looks at our charts. He points and says, "As you come up here, hang on this side, here. There's a whole island that's not there no more. You can go that way, or this way. When the wind ain't blowing, you can see the channel. But on the right side, there's a stump and a tree or two. So hang to the left side, but not too close to shore. That's where the trees are down, and you can lose your props there. So hang on this side here, then cut back over here, but watch out for the rocks! This here has all changed."

Bill looks confused and unhappy.

Bob asks, "Do you think the canoe will do better than our big boat?"

"Might," says the river rat.

When we leave, Bill says, "I guess we better stay with the canoe."

54

In the mists at Washburn

June 6, 10:00 A.M. A heavy fog sits over the river. I'm on the motor today. When Bill and I pull away from the dock at Washburn, the fog burns off quickly in the bright sun. I steer the boat close up to the cut banks where the river is swift and deep. Then I cross over to the other side, trying to follow the elusive channel. On this stretch of river, we find hunting cabins and lots more Canada geese. Two men who work for the Corps of Engineers have dragged their speedboat up on a sandbar. They wave us off. They say piping plovers nest here, and we're not allowed to walk around.

Washburn

1:00 P.M. We pass the site where Lewis and Clark spent their first winter, Fort Mandan. The actual place on the eastern bank has been washed away over the years. The explorers had to spend five cold months here waiting for the ice to break up.

At the confluence of the Knife and Missouri rivers on October 26, 1804, Lewis and Clark came to the villages of the Mandan and Hidatsa Indians. More than four thousand Indians lived here. The Mandans and the Hidatsa lived in great round earthen lodges made from timber sunk into the ground

Mile 1,375—Fort Mandan, near the Knife River

Bel-lolck-mah-pick, the Bull Dance, a part of the O-kee-pa ceremony, Mandan: oil, by George Catlin. THE GRANGER COLLECTION

and covered with earthen roofs. Several families, their horses, and large quantities of food could fit inside one of these lodges. The villages were surrounded by a clay embankment and a ditch to protect them from the Sioux. The Mandan men were big and tall. Many had light complexions. (Some people used to believe the Mandans were the descendants of a legendary Welsh expedition to the New World a thousand years ago.) Most of the Mandans and Hidatsas were later wiped out by smallpox.

Lewis and Clark spent 138 days here. On December 7, the river closed up with ice. (Three days later a herd of buffalo crossed over the river without breaking through.) The explorers' boats were locked in the river ice and covered with snow. Some men got frostbite. The winter was brutal. The temperature dropped to 45 degrees below zero.

During the long winter wait, the men collected as much information as they could about the river to the north and west. Most of this information came from the Hidatsa Indians. The Hidatsa were accustomed to visiting the Rocky Mountains.

The Hidatsa chief, One-Eye, examined Clark's servant, a black man named York. One-Eye tried to rub off York's "black paint" with wet fingers.

Lewis and Clark with Sacagawea, 1805.
THE GRANGER COLLECTION

During the winter, Lewis and Clark met a Frenchman named Charboneau. His wife was a Shoshone, sixteen or seventeen years old. She had been captured as a girl near the Rocky Mountains by a Hidatsa war party. Her name was Sacagawea, which possibly meant "Bird Woman" in Hidatsa. (Some people pronounce her name "Sacajewea." Most scholars agree, however, that her name was pronounced more like Sa-ka-ga-wea.)

Lewis and Clark hired Charboneau and his wife. Sacagawea might be useful to them when they reached the Rockies, because she could speak to the Shoshones. Maybe she would convince her people to help the expedition, which needed horses to cross the big mountains. On February 11, 1805, Sacagawea gave birth to a boy.

In late March the river ice began to break up, and on April 7, 1805, Lewis and Clark and a party of thirty-two people left Fort Mandan to travel upriver into the great unknown. With them went Sacagawea and her tiny child. Few white men had ever gone upriver from here. They traveled in six dugout canoes and two larger pirogues. The keelboat could not travel in the shallower water, so it was sent back to St. Louis.

Fort Mandan April 7, 1805
This little fleet, although not quite so respectable as those of Columbus or Captain Cook, were still viewed by us with as much pleasure. We were now about to penetrate a country at least two thousand miles in width, on which the foot of civilized man had never trodden. I could but esteem this moment of my departure as among the most happy of my life.

Stanton, North Dakota

1:45 P.M. We find a little store in Stanton, North Dakota, on the Knife River. A man from Stanton says the courthouse here was built over a Hidatsa village. He says lots of people have found buffalo skulls buried in the silt and sand of the river. He himself has found skulls when he goes scuba diving in the Missouri River. Even today buffalo skulls are used in Indian ceremonies.

At the nearby Knife River Indian Villages Historic Site, a buffalo display shows how important this animal was to the Indians of the Plains. The bladder was made into pouches; the hooves into rattles; the stomach into containers; the paunch into water buckets; the lining of the heart into waterproof wrappers; the bones into paintbrushes and tools and hoes; the horns into cups and ladles; the skull into ceremonial objects;

the tanned hides into clothes, tipi covers, robes, blankets, bags, and pouches; the hair into pillow stuffing; the flesh into meat; the rawhide into containers, shields, rope, moccasins, drumheads, bull boats, and belts. The list goes on. Even dried

buffalo droppings—chips—were made into baby powder or burned as fuel.

8 P.M. At dinner, we raise our glasses. "Here's to one more day on the river."

CHAPTER NINE

Heading West Again to the Yellowstone

June 7, 11:00 A.M. It's too blustery to get on Lake Sakakawea, our fifth big lake. In North Dakota, people say, "If you don't like the weather, wait an hour." But it looks as if we might have to wait at least another day. When the wind came up last night, it came suddenly. The temperature dropped thirty degrees. My little tent nearly flew away in the storm.

Mile 1,391, Pick City, North Dakota, Garrison Dam

Bill and I have lots of time to catch up on our notes and read the journals of Lewis and Clark. Resting is nice, but we all feel anxious to get moving again. Bill fears we might be stuck here for days waiting out the wind.

Bill working on his journal

3:00 P.M. I call home. Walker tells me to come home. Then Suzanna takes the phone. She says I have to come see her in the school play. "Daddy, I'm playing a cricket in the wetlands. My friend Abby is a waterstrider. You *have* to come see it."

I would if I could, Suzanna.

June 8, 11:15 A.M. The wind is strong but not as bad as yesterday. We launch the *Nikawa* on Lake Sakakawea—five miles wide here. So far, we've been heading north. Now the river begins its long stretch westward. I'm on Bronco duty.

Lake Sakakawea

2:00 P.M. High on a bluff overlooking the big lake, I stand on top of the canoe, on top of the Bronco. In the immense lake,

Indian Hills Campground

61

Grizzly bear growling. © Michael Deyoung/Alaska Stock Images

the *Nikawa* is a tiny speck. I wave my flag. Over the radio comes an angry voice, "Are you standing on top of the canoe, Peter?"

"Bill wants you to get down. Immediately! Or there might be a *court-martial.*"

When Lewis and Clark were at this place, they saw large grizzly tracks. They had heard of the famous beast from the Indians, but had not seen one.

Saturday, April 13, 1805
The Indians give a very formidable account of the strength and ferocity of this animal, which they never dare to attack but in parties of six, eight, or ten persons; and [they] are even then frequently defeated with the loss of one or more of their party. This animal is said more frequently to attack a man on meeting with him, than to flee from him. When the Indians are about to go in quest of the white bear . . . they paint themselves and perform all those superstitious rights commonly observed when they are about to make war upon a neighboring nation.

Mile 1,481—Four Bears Casino, Fort Berthold Indian Reservation, New Town, North Dakota

4:00 P.M. I've never planned any of my journeys as well as Bill has planned this one. He's been planning it for years. He drove every part of his transcontinental route. Even now he remembers every ramp, every hotel, every restaurant he wants to eat

The bridge at Fort Berthold Reservation

in. Tonight Bill has planned to be in the casino hotel on the Fort Berthold Indian Reservation.

Three tribes live together here. The Arikara, Hidatsa, and Mandan are descendants of some of the same Indians Lewis and Clark wintered with 190 years ago. A man named Delano tells me there's disagreement among the tribes. "Yes," he says smiling, "we were enemies in the old days."

Near the casino, a replica of an earthen lodge is under construction.

The frame for an earthen lodge

63

Lake Sakakawea

Mile 1,540—Somewhere on Lake Sakakawea

June 9, 3:00 P.M. Lake Sakakawea is yellow brown. The color comes from the huge amount of silt-laden water entering from the Yellowstone River, some forty or fifty miles north of here.

We notice something strange up ahead. A wall of brownish red vegetation runs from shore to shore, blocking any further advance. It looks as if the lake just ends. My heart begins to pound.

A wall of willow reeds stands three feet above the water. I take a pole and sound the depth. Even among the reeds it's over seven feet deep. We motor slowly through the reeds searching for the channel. The current is strong; white pelicans everywhere.

We are lost. We can't find the channel at all. We could wander in these reeds for hours. So we pull over to shore. I climb the riverbank, and, thank goodness, I stumble across a house and a man working in his garden. After he explains where the channel runs, we head slowly back into the reeds and immediately are swallowed up again. But this time we find the channel. Seems like luck.

Lost on the Missouri

6:00 P.M. Around the boat ramp in Williston, the river is a torrent with boils and all kinds of drift. We are so late, Scott has been really worried. He almost panicked and sent out a rescue plane to search the river for us.

At dinner, Bill says, "We almost forgot. Here's to surviving one more doggone day on this wacky river."

Tomorrow we reach the Yellowstone! What a name! And what an accomplishment to have gotten this far!

Mile 1,550—Williston

June 10, 1:45 P.M. The run to the Yellowstone River is only thirty miles, yet the *Nikawa* fights the current, which sends big cottonwoods downstream like torpedoes. The yellowish-brown water is wild with boils. We can actually see the silt swirling. On the surface float huge cakes of brown foam. We pass bluffs a hundred feet high. Pelicans soar from sandbar to sandbar. A white-tail deer lies down in the shade of a tree, watching us pass. We keep our eyes out for pronghorn antelope,

Mile 1,584—Confluence of Yellowstone and Missouri rivers

Junction of the Yellowstone and the Missouri, Karl Bodmer (1809-1893). Joslyn Art Museum, Omaha, Nebraska

but haven't seen any yet.

At the mouth of the Yellowstone River, Bill comes alive with excitement. "Wooo, that's the Yellowstone!" he shouts. "That's the line! Look at that!" Bill steers the *Nikawa* along the mud line where the two rivers meet.

"And look over there!" Bill shouts again. "That's green Missouri water." Just above the confluence, the Missouri turns dark green.

Scott says, "The water's alive!"

At this place, Lewis caught the mood of the men in his journal.

Friday, April 26, 1805
All in good health and much pleased at having arrived at this long-wished for spot, and in order to add in some measure to the general pleasure . . . we ordered a dram to be issued to each person; this soon produced the fiddle, and they spent the evening with much hilarity, singing & dancing, and seemed . . . perfectly to forget their past toils . . .

4:00 P.M. At the mouth of the Yellowstone today men are fishing along the shore for paddlefish. It's the strangest kind of fishing I've ever seen—and the oddest looking fish, too. This part of the Missouri River is one of the world's last natural homes for the paddlefish, which looks something like a dinosaur fish with a long paddle or bladelike snout. It can weigh up to 120 pounds and live up to fifty years.

Paddlefish. © Jim Leibelt

A man stands on shore with a big fishing rod. He casts a silver spoonlike lure with lots of hooks into the fast-moving water, then starts to jerk and drag his lure through the water. Paddlefish won't bite a lure. The fisherman has to hook a fish that happens to be swimming by. The man tells us that only twenty-five pounds of the fish can be eaten after you throw away the bones, the paddle, and all the fat.

4:15 P.M. As soon as we pass the Yellowstone, the Missouri seems to calm down. The water turns black-green. The two shores, full of cottonwoods, run close together.

Not many people today approach Fort Union from the river. But it used to be a busy place, with steamboats and keelboats coming and going. The fort was built by John Jacob Astor's powerful American Fur Company. It controlled the trading

Scott and Bill at Fort Union

Mile 1,586—Fort Union

67

Fort Union reconstructed

economy of the Northern Plains. Assiniboin, Cree, Crow, Blackfeet, and Sioux Indians traded here peaceably.

A replica of the fort has been constructed on the foundations of the old structure. Bill says, "As close as the fort was to the water, you'd think the river would have eaten the bank away. But here it is. It's nice to know exactly where it was. There are so few things along this river that are right where they were before." The fort is surrounded by open fields. In the early days, the prairie would have been dotted with tipis, the smoke rising from cooking fires.

Front gate of Fort Union

Next to the front gate on the river side of the fort is a window hardly bigger than a foot square. It was small for security reasons. Through this tiny window, the Indians passed their furs, mostly buffalo hides. But furs from other fur-bearing animals were traded too, such as elk, deer, wolf, coyote, grey fox, red fox, grizzly bear, beaver, big horn sheep, ermine, hedgehog, muskrat, and otter. Only the chiefs were allowed into the reception room to trade. A giant fur press was located near the front gate. This machine was used to compress furs into one-hundred-pound bales for shipment to St. Louis, more than 1,500 miles downriver.

In 1837 a terrible smallpox epidemic swept through the prairie tribes and the fort. Every day cart loads of corpses were dumped over the bluff into the river. Fort Union existed here for only thirty-eight years. In 1867 Fort Union was dismantled.

PART FOUR

Montana to the
Rocky Mountains

CHAPTER TEN

Canoe Days to Fort Peck

June 11, 11:00 A.M. Mountain Time. I knew it would happen. Scott will leave us next week. He's tired of traveling.

Bill, frustrated, said he's going to throw away the river charts, because the river has changed so much. Last night, he decided we should switch back to the canoe. It would be safer.

But this morning, a U.S. Fish and Game warden says we can make it thirty-seven miles to Culbertson, Montana, in the *Nikawa*. "No problem," the guy says. So Bill changes his mind and goes against his instincts. That's when we always run into trouble. He decides now to try the big boat one more day, even though the river above the Yellowstone is really narrow.

I'm on Bronco duty today, and it makes me nervous. I head out over a dusty road, passing over the Montana border. Montana! All my life I've wanted to visit this state, the fourth largest. Mountain lions, Rocky Mountain goats, elk, and bighorn sheep still roam here. Montana seems wilder than the Dakotas, more open range than farmland.

3:00 P.M. No *Nikawa*. I've parked under the bridge here that crosses the river. It's big, wild country, but peaceful. Lots of sage and dry rocky hills. Down on the river beach, an old man sits in a folding chair, fishing. He catches mostly goldeye, a beautiful silver-scaled fish with big golden eyes. People come to swim in the river here, he tells me, but lots of people have drowned.

Fort Buford boat ramp

Fisherman with goldeye

Mile 1,621—Culbertson, Montana

On facing page: Missouri River at Mountain Palace, Arca, Montana. © John Reddy.

Sandbars everywhere

Still no *Nikawa*. I leave the shortwave radio on just in case. Soon I'll have to decide: Do I stay put and hope they get here? Or do I head out to see if they need help?

In Lewis and Clark's day, this was grizzly bear country. Near Culbertson, they had their first run-in with a grizzly, their first of many to come. Lewis wrote:

Monday, April 29, 1805
I walked on shore with one man. About 8 A.M. we fell in with two [grizzlies] both of which we wounded; one of them made his escape, the other after my firing on him pursued me seventy or eighty yards, but, fortunately, had been so badly wounded that he was unable to pursue me so closely as to prevent my charging my gun. We again repeated our fire and killed him . . . . It is a much more furious and formidable animal [than the black bear], and will frequently pursue the hunter when wounded. It is astonishing to see the wounds they will bear before they can be put to death.

4:00 P.M. The call finally comes over the radio. But getting the *Nikawa* off the river is nearly impossible. I back the Bronco up into the mud at least ten times before the *Nikawa* can ride up onto the trailer. Then the wheels get stuck and I can't get her out. The trailer sinks in the ooze, and the *Nikawa* has to back off. We try another place. Finally we put boards under the trailer wheels.

The *Nikawa* is out of the water! We holler with joy. Tomorrow we'll definitely be in the canoe. We head to a local diner for a big meal. Like most meals in North Dakota and Montana, it's steak and potatoes.

June 12, 12:30 P.M. Now the canoe days begin—150 miles to the Fort Peck Dam. Four long, tedious days of meandering river.

Mile 1,649—To Brockton, Montana

The water has turned yellow again with mud. Lots of bird life but no people. I pull out my tape recorder and speak my notes. Bill writes in his little notebook with a pen. For hours I watch him studying the shore and the sky. With his interest in

Lots of sage on the river

nature and western history, Bill sees things out here most people would not notice. A good travel writer trains his eyes to see what is not always obvious. He keeps his senses alert and asks a lot of questions. Bill is curious about everything he sees.

Two great-horned owls explode into the sky from their perches. We see beaver lodges along the bank; cottonwoods leaning; banks eroding; tons of earth caving into the water. Swallows cut the air; gulls fly above; hawks are way up high. A green snake crosses our bow. A flock of twenty white pelicans rises from the water. They glide before us like messengers.

After we enter the Fort Peck Indian Reservation, the hills seem to square off. The rock formations look like castles.

5:30 P.M. Finally we reach Brockton, Montana, a hot, little, dusty town. Bill blows his whistle to let the Bronco busters know we're here. Tomorrow, we go to Poplar, another hot, little, dusty reservation town. Scott and I will Bronco bust, thank goodness. Bob and Bill will take the canoe.

Bill studying the charts in the canoe

June 13, 5:00 P.M. We meet a man named Richard. He's part Assiniboin, part Blackfeet. He is a foreman on a nearby road crew. He tells us that when he was a kid he used to fish for northern pike in the river. With his bare hands he'd reach down and grab the ten-pound fish by the gills, then toss them up on the riverbank.

Mile 1,678—Poplar, Montana

Fishing at Wolf Point

Sturgeon. Courtesy of Dr. John Ferrell, U.S. Army Corps of Engineers

June 14, 4:00 P.M. These hot canoe days are frustrating. We feel as if we're not moving anywhere, but rather just standing still, baking in the Montana sun. Bob and I find the river and wait for Scott and Bill. One fisherman named Kirt is a tall Sioux with long black hair in a ponytail. Kirt uses a spinning rod and worm. First he catches a walleye. He casts again and reels in a white bass. On his next cast, he hooks a sturgeon, then a buffalo.

Mile 1,708—Wolf Point, Montana

Kirt catches a sturgeon.

"Wow. You catch this many fish all the time?" I ask. Kirt laughs. "Nope," he says. "This is the first time I've come here."

Kirt says he won't swim in the river. It's too dangerous. "See those boils? This river has taken a few lives," says Kirt as he casts again. He doesn't speak Lakota, the Sioux language. I ask if any of the reservation children study Lakota. He says classes are offered, but not many kids have an interest.

The Assiniboins and Fort Peck

June 15, 10:00 A.M. At breakfast our waitress warns us to wear life jackets. She says, "Watch out for whirlpools! Even horses drown in the Missouri whirlpools."

Ken Ryan joins us for breakfast. He is a large, round-faced, intelligent man.

Ken was Tribal Chairman of the Assiniboins from 1984-1987. He says there are four thousand Assiniboins here on the reservation and more than 25,000 Assiniboins altogether in Montana and Canada. Most people know nothing about his tribe, he says. Even Lewis and Clark came to Ken's tribe with preconceived ideas about them.

Wolf Point, Fort Peck Reservation

Ken Ryan

Friday, May 10, 1805
We still believe ourselves in the country usually hunted by the Assiniboins, and as they are a vicious, ill-disposed nation, we think it best to be on our guard.

The Assiniboins, Ken tells us, are one of the most progressive tribes in America. Fort Peck Assiniboins are doctors, dentists, nurses, FBI agents, judges, and college teachers.

"We are not a fighting people. My mom's great-great-grandfather was taken to Washington, D.C., in 1837 by President Andrew Jackson. His name was Delight. He spent a year with the whites. They took him to New York City, to Annapolis, and to West Point. When he came back, he told our tribe, 'We should never ever fight these white people. They are like ants in an anthill. There aren't enough Assiniboins to kill all the white people.'"

I ask Ken how he got his Irish last name.

Ken's granddad was named His Black Horse. When the army came, he would not tell the white men his Indian name. He had been warned, "If they find out your Indian name, then

Fort Union on the Missouri, after Karl Bodmer, (1809-1893). Joslyn Art Museum, Omaha, Nebraska

they can keep you. But if you don't tell them your name, they can't keep you."

So the whites gave Ken's grandfather the name of Thomas Ryan. Ken's Indian name is also His Black Horse, just like his granddad's. Ken's tone is only slightly bitter. He speaks softly, with wisdom in his voice. He says he doesn't hate America. He himself served in the military. But he is critical of the way his tribe was handled from the beginning.

Ken says, "They couldn't believe that this vast expanse of land was owned by only eleven thousand Indians. So they embarked upon a policy to destroy our economic system . . . . They destroyed the Indian's food base, the buffalo. In the winter of 1884, nine hundred Assiniboins starved to death here at Wolf Point. You won't find that in any history books!

"In 1886, President Cleveland sent emissaries to our tribe. They came saying, 'You know, your Great White Father absolutely, totally, truly loves you. He cares about you and your well-being. And he wants to feed you. He doesn't like to see you starve.'

"The other thing the white people said was, 'Your Great White Father wants you to give your brothers, the white man, some of your land. You have so much land, and you never ever use it all. So you must sign this paper here and your White Father, who loves you, will feed you.'

"And that's when the Fort Peck Reservation was set up. They said the Great White Father was giving this land to us. But it was never his to give in the first place."

Until 1930 every school-age child was taken from the Fort Peck Reservation and sent thousands of miles away to boarding schools. Ken's grandma was sent to Pennsylvania at the age of fourteen; Ken's grandpa was sent off at the age of ten. The whites told the Indian children they had to be

Christians. They told the children that their grandpas and grandmas were ugly. They said the children had to learn to act like white people. They cut their braids and took away their buckskins. They made them learn English. They beat the children and washed their mouths out with soap if they spoke Assiniboin. They terrorized the children and broke their family laws. Until 1978, Ken says, Indians could not practice their religion without fear of being thrown in prison.

Ken learned most of what he knows about the Assiniboin way of life from his uncles, not his father. They taught him about tracking animals, about rattlesnakes, about the Missouri River, too.

"I first swam in the river when I was four or five. To us," he says, "the river is alive. We have a prayer about the Missouri River. I was taught the prayer as a little boy. The first time we see the river, we are taught to say, *Mini Shose, Muddy Waters, it is good to see you.* When we leave the river, we say, *Missouri River, Mini Shose, Muddy Waters, I will see you again.* My grandpa taught me if I would say this every time I saw the river, I would never die in the river."

As a boy Ken was taught how to handle a Missouri River whirlpool. He says you have to ride it down, all the way down. Ken finishes his breakfast, "Well, I sure would like to go with you on your journey." His own band of Assiniboins is called "Wadopon" or Canoe Paddlers. They hunted in Montana and the Canadian prairies of Alberta, Manitoba, and Saskatchewan. Every three years they would take a load of furs by canoe to Hudson Bay to trade them—a journey of more than a thousand miles to the east.

Ken's eyes are bright. He says with a smile, "And we have often talked about making that trip one of these days. You might be invited along, Peter."

11:30 A.M. When I look at the Missouri this morning, I say: *Mini Shose, it is good to see you.* Bill and I hop into the canoe for another long, hot day to Frazer. I'm on the motor again.

Lunch break on the hot river

2:00 P.M. Rapids ahead. We hug the south shore. I run the motor on full throttle, but we're hardly moving. At one point we have to paddle, and my paddle breaks. But ever so slowly the engine drives us forward. At times we can almost reach out and touch the bank. The roots of large cottonwood trees lie exposed, where the bank is being washed out from under them.

4:00 P.M. The sky darkens. A big storm sweeps over us. Streak lightning blasts the sky. It's not smart to be out on water when lightning is near. The thunder is like cannons firing in the west.

The wind picks up in great gusts. Bill doesn't want to get off the river. He shakes a fist at the sky. Now it's raining huge drops. The air must be 40 degrees and plummeting. We hit deadheads and sandbars in the darkening river.

I pull the canoe over to shore. The wind tries to lift the canoe. The waves are bashing the riverbank. Hailstones shoot from the sky.

Five minutes later, the storm is over. The sky clears, the sun blazes, and Bill says, "That's the Great Plains for you." Bill looks down at the mud and spots two eagle feathers. "Good omens," he says.

We empty the water out of the canoe and head on. A dead cow floats in the river stinking the air with rot. Lewis and Clark wrote often about the stench of dead buffalos.

In 1805 grizzly bears were common on this stretch of the river. Wouldn't it be great to see a grizzly on shore! Or would it?

5:00 P.M. Bill blows his whistle. Bob waves to us from the bank. And the long day is done.

Mile 1,742—Frazer Rapids

Bob and Bill

June 16, 1:00 P.M. Scott and I drive down dusty ranch roads to look at the Frazer rapids. After we see their size, we advise Bob and Bill by radio to portage— carry the canoe— around the rocks. Bill wants to run the whitewater. I'm happy when he changes his mind.

82

5:00 P.M. Scott and I drive on to Fort Peck. Hours pass until the little canoe comes into sight. Bill is angry. He says some bad things about the river. Heat mirages have played tricks on their eyes. Bill couldn't read the river because of the glare. We're all tired of this kind of travel, and we crave the mountains.

Mile 1,770—Fort Peck, Montana, Fort Peck Dam

Lewis and Clark and their men were also tired of the long, hot days in this flat terrain.

Thursday, May 9, 1805
The river . . . is much shallower or I should begin to despair of ever reaching its source . . . I begin to feel extremely anxious to get in view of the Rocky Mountains.

5:30 P.M. We lift the canoe on top of the Bronco and head for the old Fort Peck Hotel. After we pull away from the river, I realize I've forgotten to say "Mini Shose, Muddy Waters, I will see you again." I want to say the prayer every day, not because I'm afraid of drowning, although that's part of it. But I have learned that it helps to respect a great river like the Missouri. The Assiniboin prayer is a form of respect.

June 17, 10:00 A.M. We're taking the day off. It will be Bill's fifty-seventh day on America's rivers. Three quarters of his trip is complete. Out of those fifty-seven river days, he has hardly rested at all. Bill wants to catch up on his notes. I want to read and call home.

Fort Peck Dam

The old hotel we're staying in was built during the Great Depression, during construction of the Fort Peck Dam, the last of the six big Missouri dams. It is truly the biggest dam I have ever seen—the fourth largest in the world. It stretches four miles across the Missouri River Valley.

I call home, and it's the same old story. Walker cannot speak to me for very long. He begins to cry. I'm really missing home now, and a small part of me would like to get off the river, and go home.

Mile 1,877—Musselshell River, Crooked Creek Campground, Fort Peck Lake, Charles M. Russell Preserve

June 18, Father's Day, 12:00 P.M. We put the *Nikawa* into Fort Peck Lake on the other side of the dam. Bob, Scott, and Bill head off into thunderclouds for the hundred-mile run to Crooked Creek Campground. It's going to be a hard day of Bronco busting for me. Few roads lead down to this immense reservoir. The terrain has changed, too. Trees are scarce.

The Little Rockies

I see the Little Rockies, a small isolated group of mountains, in the distance. They are sacred to the Assiniboins and other Montana Indians. I can understand why. They are so lovely in the distance, so noble. They rise out of the flat land like gods.

4:30 P.M. Crooked Creek Campground. There isn't a town for fifty miles in any direction. I am hoping to find the *Nikawa*, but there is no boat in sight when I reach the water.

6:45 P.M. A crazy canoeist is repacking his gear by the water, and I chat with him. His beard and hair are thick and wild. He carries all his drinking water with him. Among his gear, he shows me an Indian hatchet he found, a sharpened stone. He's heading to New Orleans, more than three thousand miles away! His overloaded aluminum canoe looks heavy and slow. Three nights ago a great big cottonwood fell over from an eroding bank and nearly crushed him. Yesterday he shot a rattler. I envy him—to travel *downstream* in silence! And alone!

The crazy canoeist

But where's the *Nikawa*? It's hours late now.

Here on the fourteenth of May, 1805, Lewis and Clark had one of their scariest run-ins with a grizzly. Six men sneaked up on him. Four fired at once and two held back. All four bullets entered the animal. Two bullets passed through his lungs. Suddenly the bear charged. The other two men fired. One bullet broke the grizzly's shoulder, but it kept charging. Two men jumped in a canoe to escape. The other four scattered and hid in the willows to reload. They fired again. The bear charged once more. It got close to two men, so they jumped off a twenty-foot bank into the river. The grizzly jumped in, too. Another man from the bank finally shot the bear in the head and killed it.

7:00 P.M. Finally the *Nikawa* arrives! They've had a rough day in pounding waves. Once it blew so hard, they pulled to shore and waited for the wind to drop.

Bill's going to sleep on board tonight. After we set up our tents and cook dinner, I walk down to the lake. Heat lightning flashes against the darkening sky. I can picture Lewis and

Clark and their men camping here for two days. Coyotes yip in the distance. It's an eerie sound. I cast my fishing line into the lake, but with no luck. This is the heart of the wilderness of Montana. I hope someday my children can see this.

The *Nikawa* at Crooked Creek

The Missouri River Breaks: Badlands and White Rocks

June 19, 9:00 A.M. This morning, I remember: *Mini Shose, Muddy Waters, it is good to see you.* We put the canoe on board the *Nikawa*. It sits across the stern of the big boat like a silver wing. We'll run the *Nikawa* as far as she will go. When it gets too shallow, Bill and I will hop over the side into the canoe. Bob and Scott will then pilot the *Nikawa* back to the shore, where they will trailer it.

Mile 1,922—To Kipp Landing at the Robinson Bridge

The *Nikawa* with our canoe slung across its stern.

2:00 P.M. The mosquitoes are so bad we have to wear our rain gear. But somehow they find our necks, our hands, our ankles. The day is so long and hot in such a rainless and barren land,

Wild roses in bloom

I want to jump into the river and give up. We smell the perfume of wild roses in bloom, just as Lewis described in his journal. For hours, not a single road in sight, not one person. Just some cattle drinking river water and a few abandoned log cabins.

Abandoned cabin

4:00 P.M. Bill and I reach the Robinson Bridge at last! As we come up to the bridge, a powerful wind sloshes the river into mad whitecaps. A sudden gust blows Bill's hat into the water. His new $210 sunglasses are caught in the strap of the hat. Bill screams at the sky and pounds the side of the canoe. I make as tight a turn as I dare to in the big waves. Bill plucks out his hat.

By some miracle, the glasses are still hanging from the strap.

We find Bob and pull the canoe out. "Muddy Waters," I chant to myself, "I will see you again." Then we drive to a town for a good meal.

June 20, 8:30 A.M. Something feels really odd. Scott has left us.

Before the rest of us were awake, Scott drove the Bronco with the *Nikawa* and the canoe to our next destination, Virgelle. From there he'd try to get a ride to Great Falls to catch a plane home. Bill kept saying to Scott that if he left now, he'd miss the White Cliffs, perhaps the most beautiful part of the whole Missouri! But Scott wanted to get home more than he wanted to see the White Cliffs. So now it's just the three of us. I miss him already.

Above the Fred Robinson Bridge, a 149-mile segment of the Missouri has been designated a National Wild and Scenic River. It is protected and preserved in its natural, free-flowing state. It is very nearly the exact river that Lewis and Clark saw two hundred years ago. This part of the Missouri is managed by the U.S. Bureau of Land Management, called BLM for short. Motorboats are not allowed to go upriver at this time of year.

Heading into the Badlands

Our BLM guide and pilot today is Chan Biggs. He'll take us upriver in a jet boat. We are getting VIP treatment because Bill is a well-known writer. But Bill thinks it is funny that we can't take a little canoe with a little motor on this scenic river, yet the government will take us in a faster and louder boat. Nevertheless, Bill is thankful for the lift. We'll just be tourists for once. In two days we'll cover what might have taken us five days in our canoe.

Lewis and Clark spent twenty days on this part of the river.

Chan Biggs driving the jet boat

10:00 A.M. Chan Biggs picks us up, trailering his jet boat. Chan is a rugged-looking man, a cowboy in an official tan uniform. His hair is short and bristly, a military cut. Chan laughs heartily and smiles a good deal. He says his jet boat helps in river rescues because it can go in such shallow water. "I've bagged seven bodies on this river. Each one has died from one of two things," he says brusquely. "Either no life jacket or careless behavior."

"Jet boat" sounds pretty fancy, but it is a regular flat-bottomed boat with a 115 horsepower Mercury outboard. The engine has no propeller. Instead it pushes out a jet of air into the water. The jet itself sits only a few inches under water. We have forty gallons of fuel. The engine gets maybe two or three miles per gallon, so we'll have to refuel at Judith Landing, sixty-one miles upriver.

12:00 P.M. The engine takes awhile to fire up. Then away we zoom at fifteen miles per hour, which seems much faster than the *Nikawa* because the river is so narrow. Pelicans scatter before our loud, sudden appearance. The ever-present boils well up and kick us around.

1:00 P.M. These are the Badlands, so named by the fur traders for their harshness. The towering cliffs rise straight out of the water. Some are layered in lines of red and black and white. Chan stops the boat every once in a while to tell us some history. Here, he shows us an abandoned gold mine. There, he

90

points to a ruined cabin of some homesteader who tried to live out here alone, and failed.

Even in the 1870's—the height of the steamboat era—there were few towns along this part of the river. This was Blackfeet territory, and the Blackfeet hated whites. The few towns that did exist were semilawless places, with justice by lynching. The hills were havens for outlaws.

Lewis and Clark campsite

Chan points to the Lewis and Clark campsite of May 26, 1805. Here, Clark rendered his opinion of the Badlands:

Sunday, May 26, 1805
This country may with propriety I think be termed the Deserts of America, as I do not conceive any part can ever be settled, as it is deficient in water, timber, and too steep to be tilled. We pass old Indian lodges in the woody points every day.

View of the Bear Paw Mountains from Fort McKenzie, Karl Bodmer (1809-1893). Joslyn Art Museum, Omaha, Nebraska

Mile 1,983—Judith Landing

3:00 P.M. The man who was supposed to supply us with extra fuel cannot be found. We walk up the dirt road to his farm. He's not around, and neither are the canisters of fuel.

Chan is not exactly sure how much fuel is left in the tank, but he thinks we can make it to Virgelle, another forty-six miles. I'm not wild about the idea. Being stranded on the river without a spare motor and without sleeping gear doesn't sound like fun. Chan does have a shortwave radio on his boat, so I suppose we could be rescued. Anyway, here goes!

Upriver from Judith Landing, Lewis and Clark found the remains of "a vast many mangled carcasses of buffalo," which they believed had been driven over a 120-foot cliff by Indians. Lewis described the Indian practice of using such "buffalo jumps" along the river to hunt buffalo. A brave warrior dressed in buffalo robes would place himself between the herd and the cliff. When he gave the signal, the hunting party would charge the herd all at once, driving them toward the cliff. The decoy would run out in front of the fleeing buffalo, leading them to the precipice. When the warrior got to the edge of the cliff, he would jump away to safety, while the buffalo dove over the cliff to their deaths.

Mile 2,003—White Cliffs

Golden eagle. © Dr. E. R. Degginger

5:00 P.M. Now the land is positively magical. The cliffs on both sides of the narrow river form a canyon. Some have names like Dark Butte and Steamboat Rock. The sun slants against great walls of stone. Chan points to a golden eagle's nest high on a cliff.

Certain rock formations look like toadstools. Others resemble ancient walls. It's eerie. Not of this world.

White Cliffs of the Missouri River, Eye of the Needle (LaBarge Rock beyond).
© Chan Biggs

    Lewis said these rocks looked like the ruins of cities, massive buildings, spires, and statues:

Friday, May 31, 1805.

The hills and river cliffs, which we passed today, exhibit a most romantic appearance. The bluffs of the river rise to the height of from 2 to 300 feet and in most places nearly perpendicular. They are formed by remarkable white sandstone. . . . The water in the course of time in descending from those hills and plains on either side of the river has trickled down the soft sand cliffs and worn it into a thousand grotesque figures . . . As we passed on it seemed as if those scenes of visionary enchantment would never have an end.

The White Cliffs of the Lewis and Clark Trail. © Chan Biggs

5:35 P.M. Suddenly our engine coughs, then dies. We float quickly backward with the current. The rocks above us seem to lean in on us as if to speak.

The Missouri River has thrown us its end-of-the-day surprise. Chan tries the starter. Nothing. We drift. Chan bangs his head with his hand. He's tired.

"Well," he says. "Guess we're out of gas." Chan laughs half-heartedly. "Guess this engine doesn't get three miles a gallon."

We had all hoped for a good dinner in Virgelle. But we're twenty-six miles away, and we have no food in the boat.

8:00 P.M. We've been waiting hours for help. Chan has been in touch over the radio with someone from his office in Fort Benton. The man is trying to reach us, but the old dirt road down to the river has been washed out long ago.

We're just downriver from Dark Butte. Nearby, there's a falling-down log cabin. The map says this is Sheep Shed Coulee. It's a desolate, haunting place. Bill climbs the nearby

Sheep Shed Coulee 20 miles past Judith Landing; 26 miles from Virgelle

Out of gas near Sheep Shed Coulee

hills to look out for the rescue car. I take pictures of prairie dogs. Just as Lewis and Clark said, these "barking squirrels" dive into their holes when I approach.

A golden eagle has some small animal in its talons. The final rays of the sun die on the cliffs across the river. The air grows cold. A meadowlark sings its last lonely song. The cliffs turn suddenly to a dark brown. We sit and wait and get a disappointing message over the radio. The man with the fuel is not able to reach us.

9:00 P.M. We've decided to drift back five miles to a recently occupied homestead. Perhaps the rescue car can reach that place. Chan hangs his head with fatigue. Bob, Bill, and I take turns with the paddles. We try to keep this big awkward boat

Bob and Bill paddle the jet boat.

over near the shore. Not easy. Even so, I love traveling without the motor. This is my first time with no motor in a journey of 1,300 river miles. We can hear the cottonwood leaves rustling as we pass.

When we reach the homestead, Bill and I go have a look. It's strange. The door is open. Bottles and cans still sit on the shelves. Now the rescue car shows up. We refuel with difficulty. Chan has decided to run the river in the dark, something no steamboat pilot would ever do.

10:00 P.M. We're racing into the last glimmer of light in the western sky. The jet engine seems louder at night. Chan reads the river by looking quickly from side to side. He knows the river well and seems a kind of river hero, standing tall in the cold wind, peering into the dark. The rest of us bundle into our rain gear to keep warm. The dark cliffs on either side seem to lean forward and say, "Go back. Go back to where you came from!"

For two freezing dark hours we fly on a black river through a dark canyon of invisible rock. Suddenly in the sky the northern lights shimmer. The air fills with the sharp smell of Ponderosa pine.

Midnight. We are almost at Virgelle. Chan is having a hard time seeing the river because of the dial lights on the control panel. To put the lights off, he hits a button. Suddenly the motor is silent, hugely silent, and we begin to drift once more. A fuse has blown.

We paddle in the dark to shore, right into a group of canoeists. We rouse them from their tents. They say they will watch the boat. Chan says we're at a place called Little Sandy. We have to trust him.

So now four, cold, weary travelers begin a hike. We stagger up, up, out of the river bottom and onto the high plains. We head west following the stars. Chan says he knows where we're going. But it's a nightmare of barbed wire fences and mud puddles. We pass herds of nervous cattle, phantom shapes in starlight.

After Chan's flashlight runs out of batteries, my little flashlight is all we have. Chan looks dangerously tired. He begins to stumble. Bill, Bob, and I worry about him. I have an extra apple for just such an emergency. I cut Chan a slice. I offer to take his big pack on my shoulders.

We keep following the stars to the west. Virgelle is to the west. We walk for hours. We stumble onward not knowing if we're anywhere near our goal.

Bob cheerfully prods us onward, reassuring us we're headed in the right direction. When the chips are down, a perky person like Bob can make all the difference. But as the hours pass, even Bob grows less optimistic. Lights on the plains are deceptive. They seem close, but are many miles away. Often they disappear altogether.

We begin to lose hope. At one point Bill drops to the ground for a rest and falls immediately to sleep. We rouse him and off we go. More cattle lowing in the darkness. More barbed-wire fences. The night seems endless.

June 21, 4:30 A.M. Just when Bill and I are about to lie down for what is left of the night, we spot the river lights of Virgelle. Far below. We must have walked eight miles in four hours.

Mile 2,029—Virgelle, Montana

June 21, Noon. Last night's river trip was foolish perhaps. We could easily have hit a canoeist out for a night paddle or a log that would have flipped us over at that speed.

98

Virgelle is a town of only a few buildings. Don Sorensen runs canoe trips from Virgelle through the White Cliffs. His base is a 1912 general store that once provided ranchers and railroad workers with supplies. Don once spent seven winter days stuck in his building before the road crew could plow him out of twelve-foot-high snow drifts.

Virgelle Mercantile. © Don Sorenson

1:00 P.M. While Chan works on the motor, Bob takes pictures of tipi rings. These are rocks in a circle that were used to hold down the buffalo hides of the tipi. They've been sitting in the brush for more than a hundred years, holding down phantom tipis. Here, the old west seems close to our own time.

Mile 2,070—Fort Benton, Montana

Tipi rings. © Bob Lindholm

June 22, 10:00 A.M. Chan got us to Fort Benton yesterday. Fort Benton was—and is still—one of the few river towns along the upper Missouri. Amazingly well preserved, this little town looks much as it did in the steamboat days.

Fort Benton saw its first steamboat in 1859. That's when the town became the head of navigation, meaning that it was the farthest steamboats could travel on the Missouri. Steamboats could not go beyond Fort Benton because of a series of waterfalls upriver.

The peak year for river traffic was 1879. Forty-seven steamboats reached Fort Benton that year, and the town boomed. The days of the fur trade were over, but gold had been discovered in the northern Rockies. Miners would arrive in Fort Benton, then head out overland to their claims. Some of the steamboats that left Fort Benton taking gold downriver hit snags and sank. Some of these have never been found. Sitting in an old river channel somewhere, buried under tons of silt, they wait for future treasure hunters to find them.

Steamboat "DeSmet" at Fort Benton levee, circa 1890. Montana Historical Society, Helena, Montana

Good Missouri River pilots were in great demand. One steamboat captain wrote, "We used to separate the men from the boys at the mouth of the Missouri. The boys went up the Mississippi and the men went up the Missouri."

7:00 P.M. Tonight the river is running ten miles per hour, too fast for our canoe. So we run up to the rapids at Belt Creek in a jet boat. It's as far as we can go. Many have died in these rapids. It is here that Lewis and Clark began their sixteen-mile portage around the Great Falls of the Missouri.

CHAPTER THIRTEEN

Great Falls and Gates of the Mountains

June 23, 2:00 P.M. We explore the Great Falls on foot. They are magnificent, as they were in Lewis's day. But now a spillway has been built along the top of the falls and a hydroelectric power plant. Just upriver there are four more waterfalls, nearly as large.

We drive the *Nikawa* around them. You cannot canoe this part of the river, unless you have a death wish.

Mile 2,120—Great Falls, Montana

The Great Falls of the Missouri

Lewis and Clark knew that when they found the Great Falls, they were close to the Rockies and on the right trail. On June 13, 1805, Lewis overlooked a beautiful plain, fifty or sixty miles wide. He saw more buffalo than he'd ever seen. Then he noticed something that gave him great pleasure.

Thursday, June 13, 1805
I had proceeded about two miles with Goodrich at some distance behind me when my ears were saluted with the agreeable sound of a fall of water. And advancing a little further, I saw the spray arise above the plain like a column of smoke....I soon [heard] a roaring too tremendous to be mistaken for any cause short of the great falls of the Missouri.

Even though he was sick, Lewis was so excited he could hardly describe what he saw. He wished he could be a great artist or a great writer to capture the beauty of the falls.

The next day, on June 14, Lewis climbed a hill and gazed at the snow-clad Rockies, the real Rockies. He shot a buffalo, and then suddenly was attacked by a grizzly. His rifle was unloaded. The bear ran at him with an open mouth. Lewis dashed eighty yards to the river, where he plunged in. Fortunately, the bear turned around and left.

Portaging the falls with all their gear was extremely difficult for the explorers. Wheels were built for the canoes. The wind was so strong they hoisted a sail and actually "sailed on dry land." The expedition spent a horrible month carrying around the falls and preparing to move upriver. It was extremely hot. Prickly pear thorns penetrated their moccasins. The men limped and fainted. At night they fell asleep instantly, exhausted. Yet they remained cheerful and uncomplaining.

A prickly pear cactus

June 23, 5:00 P.M. A stroke of luck. A man named Jim Pierce is willing to run us up the river in his jet boat, this evening! The plan is to leave the *Nikawa* and the Bronco in the city of Great Falls. Jim will take Bob and Bill, and I'll follow in Jim's pickup truck with his trailer. When we reach Holter Dam, we'll trailer the jet boat back to where we started, back to Great Falls.

Mile 2,120—Great Falls, Montana

Jim owns a car dealership in Great Falls. He's glad to help, because he loves jet boating. His Thunder Jet can run us the ninety miles to Holter Dam in a few hours. In our canoe this distance would take three whole days! It's a brand new jet boat, three times faster than Chan Bigg's boat, and built for running fast, shallow rivers. It looks like a mean machine, too—all fiberglass with a canvas sunroof. It has cabin heat, windshield wipers, flood lights, and a CB radio.

Jim says his boat runs forty-five miles per hour against a six-mile-an-hour current! So I'll be flying to keep up. I envy Bob and Bill. They get to ride in this high-tech wonder.

7:00 P.M. I can see the snow in the Rockies off to the south-west. The Missouri heads straight toward them. The river can't be a hundred yards wide here. (Not a lot of space to maneuver a fast boat!)

Rushing down the road, I pass through lovely hill farms and cattle ranches. Then the road winds up into the foothills of the Rockies. Pine, balsam, and cedar trees grow at strange

angles out of the rock buttresses. The terrain grows rugged—
volcanic. This is definitely no longer the plains. The river has
turned again to a dark green color. We're getting close to the
river's source; I can feel it!

**Mile 2,210—Nearing
Holter Dam**

8:00 P.M. The road climbs steeply, following the very edge of the river. At times I drive so close to Jim's Thunder Jet, I can wave at them and they wave back. Or I race ahead to stop, jump out of the truck, and take photos as they pass.

Pronghorn antelope herd. R. & D. Aitkenhead/Animals Animals

Pronghorn antelope feed on the green hillsides. The summer evening light slants across fishing dories as they drift downstream. This portion of river is a blue ribbon trout stream. Fly fisherman don't like speed boats, so Jim slows as he passes them.

Holter Dam is small by comparison to anything we've seen. On the other side is Holter Lake, also small by comparison. But that's for tomorrow's journey.

I back Jim's trailer down a ramp, and he drives the Thunder Jet onto the trailer. Jim's happy about the run. We're all abuzz, too. Painless—no Missouri River surprises! What a boat!

Mini Shose, I will see you again.

10:00 P.M. Tonight, we toast the river, and Bill makes a prediction. "Peter," he says, "I predict you will someday come out west to live." I wonder if Bill is right. I've fallen in love with the land, the sky, this river, and the good people we've met along our route. But I can feel home pulling me back east, too.

Day off in Great Falls

June 24, 9:00 A.M. Today we have time to explore the city of Great Falls and visit the museum of the pioneer cowboy artist Charles Russell. Charlie Russell was a Missouri River painter. In the 1800's many artists came to paint the river—Karl

106

C.M. Russell, "Buffalo in Winter," 1912, oil on board, C.M. Russell Museum, Great Falls, Montana

Bodmer, George Catlin, John Audubon. But only Russell lived his life around it. He came to Montana at the age of sixteen. For a while he was a trapper and traded his furs at Fort Benton. Then he worked on a cattle ranch. During the long winters, like the terrible winter of 1886-87, when the horns of the cattle exploded with cold, Russell began to paint.

June 25, 11:00 A.M. Bill and I are back in the *Nikawa* today. We'll travel almost due south now. We're very near the capital of Montana, Helena. We still have to trailer around three dams: Holter Dam, Hauser Dam, and Canyon Ferry Dam. The small lakes that have formed behind the dams are used for recreation. It's a weekend, so there will be plenty of pleasure boats out today. Nobody headed across the country to the Pacific Ocean, though!

Mile 2,215—Holter Lake

1:00 P.M. The Missouri is extremely narrow through this high rock canyon. Bill has to watch where he steers, to avoid other boats and people on water skis. When we pass through the Gates of the Mountains, I watch the sheer cliffs for signs of mountain goats.

Lewis and his men found this terrain gloomy. They had taken four days to get here, and still they had not made contact with the Shoshone Indians.

> *Friday, July 19, 1805*
> *The mosquitoes are very troublesome to us as usual. . . .*
> *This evening we entered much the most remarkable cliffs that we have yet seen. These cliffs rise from the water's edge on either side perpendicularly to the height of 1,200 feet. Every object here wears a dark and gloomy aspect. The towering and projecting rocks in many places seem ready to tumble on us. . . .*
> *I called it the Gates of the Mountains.*

The Gates of the Mountains. © John Reddy

The Gates of the Mountains–Missouri River
North of Helena, Montana. © John Reddy

Hauser Dam

2:00 P.M. After the amazing rock faces of the Gates of the Mountains, the land levels out into rolling hills. Dry terrain here. Dust devils rise off the plain. Many of the farmers' fields have to be irrigated. It's a far cry from the wet bottomlands on the lower river. Bob goes with the *Nikawa*, and I'm Bronco-busting for the rest of the day.

Mount Baldy and Edith and Canyon Ferry.
© John Reddy

Canyon Ferry Dam

5:00 P.M. The Bitterroot Range of the Rockies show bright and snowcapped. We're getting very close to Three Forks!

Mile 2,275—Townsend

7:00 P.M. At the far end of Canyon Ferry Lake, the water grows shallow. The river is a natural river again. Two pronghorn spring across the road. The mosquitoes are horrific. I put the trailer into the water when the *Nikawa* comes into sight.

Last Days: At Three Forks

June 26, 11:00 A.M. Walker's third birthday! I call him from a pay phone. He actually speaks with me! He's happy, because today he will get presents and cake. He says I should come home so I can open presents with him. "I'll see you in two days," I say. I feel great.

11:30 A.M. The water is really roiling under the Townsend bridge as Bill and I get into the canoe. Mosquitoes are terrible. As usual, I'm on the motor. Today we'll try to reach the very first dam on the Missouri River, the Toston irrigation dam. We

Mile 2,275—Townsend

The Three Forks of the Missouri, the meeting point of the Madison, Jefferson, and Gallatin rivers. Courtesy Dr. John Ferrell, U.S. Army Corps of Engineers

have only twenty miles to cover today, but this might take us nine hours. Bill's little motor can only push the canoe a meager few miles per hour against the force of the raging current here.

As Lewis and Clark neared Three Forks, their spirits rose. They expected any moment to meet the Shoshone. Lewis wrote:

Monday, July 22, 1805
[Sacagawea] recognizes the country and assures us that this is the river on which her relations live, and that the three forks are at no great distance. This piece of information has cheered the spirits of the party who now begin to console themselves with the anticipation of shortly seeing the head of the Missouri yet unknown to the civilized world.

3:00 P.M. We can only make headway if we travel near the banks, because there the current is a little less powerful. So I run the canoe so close that we can reach out and touch the wild roses in bloom. Bill shouts, "Now you're a Missouri River man."

6:00 P.M. The speed of the river as we approach the dam has to be ten or eleven miles per hour. Perhaps this is the snowmelt finally rolling off the mountains. A storm is coming in, stirring up the smell of sagebrush. Thunder and wind are at our backs. Bill moves suddenly to one side, and we nearly swamp. "Keep loose," I yell at him. If either of us stiffens up, our bodies will make the boat more tippy.

The boat is not making headway. I shout "Paddle!" But just then the little motor drives us

The Toston Irrigation Dam

112

slowly up around a boulder. Lightning. The sky is dark as night. Rain pelts us. On we push.

And here is the little irrigation dam and Bob with the Bronco. We pull out, and I say the prayer: *Mini Shose, I will see you again.*

9:00 P.M. Bill is worried about getting upriver tomorrow. It is twenty-five miles from the dam up to Three Forks. If the river runs just a little faster than it did today, that canoe won't make headway against the current. And it's much too shallow for the *Nikawa.*

So I'm delighted when Bill agrees we should run the canoe downstream tomorrow. In that way, we will have "covered" this part of the Missouri. I love the idea of canoeing the river the way the river wants us to go—downstream.

June 27, 11:00 A.M. We wake to grey skies. It's blustery and cold, like fall in New England. Too cold for mosquitoes. We drive to Three Forks National Park, where the Madison and the Jefferson rivers join the Missouri. Although geographically the source of the Missouri is farther upstream, Three Forks is where the Missouri begins *symbolically*. This is the very place that Lewis and Clark stood on July 25, 1805. For them, this was the beginning of the river. We take pictures of ourselves, 2,320 miles up the Missouri.

Here Lewis wrote: "The beds of all these streams are formed of smooth pebble and gravel, and their waters perfectly transparent." Here

Mile 2,320—Three Forks National Park

Bill at Three Forks National Park

113

Sacagawea pointed out the place she was captured by the Hidatsa raiding party five years before.

The author leaving Three Forks on the last day

11:20 A.M. For part of our trip today, we'll try paddling with no motor. Bill has taken the stern. We've never paddled a canoe together, and I feel a little awkward in the bow.

We're hauling downstream. It feels great. But suddenly I spot a log ahead, directly in front of us. I shout, "Paddle hard." To avoid collision, I can't help spraying Bill with my paddle.

He shouts back, "What are you doing? Why paddle so hard!"

Snappishly, I ask Bill if he realizes how close we came to tipping.

"Just slow down!" he says. Bill's as furious as a wet cat. "Listen," he blasts, "I know we haven't paddled together before. But there's only one captain on this boat. If you want to be captain, you can get out *right here.*"

I bite my tongue and bury my anger. This is the first time he's yelled at me. I feel like abandoning ship. Instead, I say, "Okay, just tell me where you want to go."

But soon the anger passes. We've come through a lot on this river.

2:00 P.M. The headwind slows us down, even with this strong current. We put away our paddles, and Bill starts the motor.

A large cliff juts into the river. I'm taking a photograph, when suddenly the boat begins to flounder. Before I know what's really happening, we're on the edge of a whirlpool the size of a small building. I yell, "Gun it!" And Bill, who has not yet seen the whirlpool, does what I ask. He fires the engine into full throttle, and we inch our way up and out of the swirling boat-eater.

Afterward, Bill says, "Thanks. I didn't even see that thing."

3:00 P.M. I switch into the stern. Going downstream, we must be running sixteen miles an hour, an incredible speed for a canoe.

We stop to investigate a long-abandoned homestead, a one-room cabin. White pelicans float like kites against the grey cliffs. The majestic birds of the upper Missouri remind

An abandoned homestead on the Upper Missouri

me of how free I feel on this incredible river.

So much has happened in the nearly two centuries since Lewis and Clark first came. Much of the wildlife has retreated to the mountains. The buffalo are mainly gone. Native Americans, once lords of this big country, are penned into relatively small patches of it. Many parts of the great river have been dammed, pegged down, and manipulated. And yet there is still wildness here, a great power only partially tied down.

We fly around a bend. The dam is in sight. Suddenly, the wind kicks up whitecaps. We spot a bald eagle in the trees.

The canoe bounces hard against the waves. The wind blows away the clouds. The sky turns blue. And here's the sun, blazing on a hundred white pelicans as they whirl over our heads to say farewell.

White pelicans at the end of our journey

Epilogue

Bill saw me to my hotel that night. I thanked him for having me along. He replied, "Thank you for your great help. I apologize for all my failings."

Bill had summed up his feelings about the Missouri a few days before. He had told me, "I've been on a lot of waterways—the Hudson, the Erie Canal, the Mohawk, the Allegheny, the Ohio, the Mississippi—and I'll be on others after this. But the Missouri is not only the longest river, it's the orneriest. It's the toughest, the most rewarding, the most frustrating—whatever the *most* is—that's it over there." And he pointed at the Muddy Waters.

"Hey, Bill," I said. "You're going to make it to the Pacific!"

"I think I'm going to make it," he said. Then he was gone.

Bill did make it. He went over the Continental Divide and rafted down the whitewater of the Salmon River. Then he got back on board the *Nikawa* and reached the Pacific Ocean on August 2, 1995. He completed his 103-day, 5,400-mile river journey across the United States in just over three months.

Lewis and Clark finally made contact with the Shoshone. Sacagawea was indeed helpful in getting her people to give the explorers horses to get over the mountains. They too finally reached the Pacific on November 6, 1805. After wintering on the coast at Fort Clatsop, now in Oregon, they returned to St. Louis the following year. They had traveled eight thousand miles in two and a half years. In so doing, they described times and places and peoples that would never again be the same.

After I got home, my son Walker wouldn't speak to me for a long time. He was so full of emotion. I held him on my chest, his head resting on my shoulder. A few days later he said he wanted to go with me on the Missouri River someday. Just the two of us. So I promised him a trip. Maybe in a few years we'll paddle a section of the White Cliffs.

Mini Shose, I will see you again.

Index